The Book of Etiquette and Manners

A comprehensive guide on good manners & courtesies

Nimeran Sahukar
&
Prem P. Bhalla

PUSTAK MAHAL®

Publishers

Pustak Mahal®

Administrative office and sale centre

J-3/16 , Daryaganj, New Delhi-110002
☎ 23276539, 23272783, 23272784 • *Fax:* 011-23260518
E-mail: info@pustakmahal.com • *Website:* www.pustakmahal.com

Branches
Bengaluru: ☎ 080-22234025 • *Telefax:* 080-22240209
E-mail: pustakmahalblr@gmail.com
Mumbai: ☎ 022-22010941, 022-22053387
E-mail: unicornbooksmumbai@gmail.com
Patna: ☎ 0612-3294193 • *Telefax:* 0612-2302719
E-mail: rapidexptn@gmail.com

© **Pustak Mahal, New Delhi**

ISBN 978-81-223-0834-1

Edition: 2016

Printed at : Radha Offset, Delhi

DEDICATION

*To Preeti, Nikhil and Cyrus,
who have no need for this book.*

*To Riya, who has yet a long
way to go...*

Preface

Down the ages, even when society was primitive, certain norms on expected behaviour patterns were laid down, which man had 3to follow. These etiquette and courtesies became integral parts of each personality where those without "manners" were branded "crude" and "uncultured", whereas people who knew how to conduct themselves on all occasions, reflected not only "good upbringing" but were also a pleasure to deal with. How we define good manners for ourselves delineates our personal boundaries of correct behaviour.

In India, love and respect – particularly for the elderly – is ingrained into our psyche in childhood. Family values are instilled during the formative years and play an integral part in shaping individuals. But despite our best efforts, ever so often, etiquette and good manners take a backseat in our list of priorities, either because it is convenient to ignore them, or there is a genuine lack of understanding about what constitutes correct behaviour and etiquette.

This book attempts to act as a guide for all those who seek specific outlines on conventional behaviour patterns and etiquette, established originally by Western tradition, which are accepted worldwide today. It defines the difference between social and business etiquette and reaffirms the ancient saying, "Manners maketh a man".

— **Nimeran Sahukar**

Contents

1

Etiquette and Manners

"Good breeding is the result of much good sense, some good nature, and a little self-denial for the sake of others, and with a view to obtain the same indulgence from them."

– Lord Chesterfield

All civilised societies are built upon discipline. To give direction to this discipline, a country adopts a constitution, and enacts laws to implement it. In the same way, a company adopts a memorandum of incorporation, a small business a partnership deed, a charity a trust deed. These documents suggest ways to handle particular situations.

Mankind is gregarious by nature. People meet each other at all levels. They are together at home, at work and in everyday life. Every individual is guided by personal needs. These may be contrary to others' needs, causing unnecessary tension and ill-will for all concerned. To overcome this, mankind adopted certain unwritten guidelines. These help create harmony in the relationships between people.

These guidelines were not adopted as one would a legal document. They are the result of innumerable suggestions from time to time. These suggestions became actions, and repeated actions became customs. These guidelines are contrary to the nature of the "animal" in man, and are not instinctive. Therefore, the habits need to be cultivated. Some sacrifices are involved. These customs reflect good manners that then transform into etiquette.

Etiquette implies adhering to conventional requirements of social behaviour. It aims at dignity for an individual and exemplifies good breeding, acceptance of morals and good taste.

Good etiquette begins with you.

Manners denote the way one acts. They reflect the style and habits of an individual and refer to one's external behaviour.

Good breeding does not come from good education alone. It comes from a person being thoughtful towards everyone, from care and consideration for others. Whenever he wishes to judge his actions, a good person asks himself a question. Is it fair to all concerned? If the answer is "yes", he goes ahead. If not, he changes direction.

In themselves, good etiquette and manners may appear to be of little importance. Life aims at one getting along well with people in everyday life. The issues are seemingly minor. Yet, it is always the people with good etiquette and manners who move ahead. They are easily accepted everywhere.

❏ ❏ ❏

2

Are You What
You Want to Be?

We never realise it, but every person is many persons in one. Your boss may have one image of you. Your colleagues quite another. Simultaneously, your subordinates may think differently about you. Your spouse and children may also have different images of you, just as your friends and relatives will.

Which of these is the real you? This is important because you may have an altogether different image of yourself. No progressive person can afford to be like this. You too would like to be considered what you think you are – a good person!

One's hopes and aspirations guide every individual. Beginning as thoughts, these turn into dreams. Dreams turn into actions. Actions become habits. The sum total of one's good and bad habits decides what a person is like. Etiquette and manners have a direct influence upon one's image. Although one's image is an outward reaction, it has much to do with one's education and upbringing. One can pretend sometimes, but not always.

Have you ever observed how a colleague will walk up to you and say, "Are you all right? You are looking very low." Or, on opening the door, your wife's first question to you is, "It appears you have had a very hard day at office. Is everything all right?" Even the children are observant. They get to know when you are happy. They will ask for favours at the right time.

There are two parts of the image you project of yourself. The first pertains to your external appearance – your health, your sense of cleanliness and dress. The second pertains to your mental development – your education, upbringing and emotional maturity. To constantly improve your image, understand yourself. Gauge your strengths and weaknesses. Enhance your strengths and overcome weaknesses.

If you want to be well accepted, your health and cleanliness should be of importance. The way you dress helps draw immediate attention. Clothes speak loudly. However, elegance of dress does not necessarily come from expensive or trendy clothes. Clean, crisp clothes worn without much fuss enhance personal charm. The secret is to dress according to the occasion.

The face is always the centre of attraction. It is also an index of one's thoughts. The power of attraction comes from thoughts. Just as happiness and gaiety attract goodwill and well-being, thoughts of anxiety, worry, anger and envy leave tell-tale marks on the face. One must be happy to radiate one's inner beauty.

Etiquette and good manners are necessarily a part of a person. They reflect his concept of morality. A good person will observe etiquette. Good manners come naturally to him. His life is based upon creating goodwill. On the other hand, a person who has a distorted view of life will fail to observe etiquette. Good manners mean nothing to him.

If you want the world to accept you as a good human being, you will have to prove through good etiquette with everyone you come across that you are a good person. Decide what you want to be. Set out to learn the skills to deal with people. Become the person you want to be.

3

Etiquette and Body Language

In dealing with people, it is not enough to rely only upon what one says. There is much that one can learn about a person's feelings and emotions by observing the body language. Gestures speak louder than words. The body reflects one's feelings. We are all aware of some gestures that are universal. A smile when one is happy, a frown when one is angry and crying when one is sad need no words to express these feelings. The shaking of the head to say yes or no is well known. Biting one's nails, shaking the legs, or tapping the table reflect nervousness. Some people keep pulling their hair. Without a word we realise that they are uneasy.

His crossed legs suggest a 'closed' attitude.

Crossing one's legs is a sign of 'closing up'. The person wants to shut out others. He does not want his privacy to be invaded at any cost. Arms crossed over the chest also convey similar feelings.

The eyes are mirrors of the soul. Eyes reflect what you feel. They express the transparency of a person. Injury, pain, joy, depression, elation and anguish are all conveyed through one's eyes. There is little need to say anything. A sensitive person perceives what the other feels by simply looking into the eyes. Have you ever been to an Indian classical dance recital? Without uttering a single word, the dancer depicts many expressions.

In one of her articles, psychologist Jane Templeton observes that if a person's eyes are downcast, and the face turned away, it means the person is trying to 'shut out' the observer. If the mouth is relaxed without a mechanical smile, and the chin is pushed forward, he is probably concentrating on a problem. If his eyes engage yours continuously with a single one-sided smile, he is weighing your proposal. If his head is at the same level as yours, the smile relaxed, and he appears to be enthusiastic, your proposal is accepted.

Another activity that reveals a great deal about one's personality is the way one walks. Everyone has a distinctive way of walking. Posture depends upon one's emotions. If a person is happy and things have gone well, the steps will be light, the arms moving in a casual manner, and the head held high. If the person is depressed and worried, the shoulders will droop, the walk will be slow, and the head will bend downwards.

Adults who walk rapidly and swing their arms freely are goal-oriented. They pursue their goals zealously. The person who walks with his hands in the pockets even in summer is prone to criticising. He is secretive and happiest when pulling someone down and glorifying himself. Such people are dangerous. There are no limits to the harm they can do.

Those who walk with their hands on the hips are the no-nonsense types. They move fast to get on with their work. *Move* – that is their key word. It is action all the way for them.

A calculated walker has an exaggerated swing. The legs are stiff and deliberate in their movements. Such a person is calculating and manipulative. He is best avoided.

The person who looks down continuously each step of the way, ensuring there are no stones, no bumps that may make him fall, is the overcautious type. He believes in thinking a hundred times before he acts.

People who walk with hands folded behind their backs are more introverted in nature. Though intelligent and hardworking, they do not relish being the centre of attraction. They prefer remaining in the shadows, rather than coming into the limelight.

Most of us are emotional by nature. We talk quickly. To support our words, we use our hands. Gestures convey more than words. Sometimes, they precede the conversation. One gesture commonly associated with sincerity and loyalty is the open hand. We use it very frequently.

When frustrated, one opens the hands and shouts. The shoulder-shrugging gesture too is followed by the open-hand gesture. This is symbolic of the open-mindedness of the person. The person has nothing to hide and is completely transparent. When children have achieved something they are proud of, they can be observed opening their hands. When it is the reverse, their hands will invariably be in their pockets. We are all aware of a handshake. All handshakes look similar, but each conveys a different meaning.

Opening and closing one's coat buttons is another indicative move. If the person opens the coat buttons, or takes off the coat, the person is extending cordial vibrations in your favour. If it is the reverse, it is an indication of ill feeling and resentment.

Charles Darwin, the British scientist, observed that dogs lie on their backs completely defenceless when they feel safe and comfortable in the presence of a person. Similarly, human beings feel relaxed when they are in congenial company.

He is lost in deep thought.

A person who cracks knuckles has a nervous disposition. When a person is in deep thought and scratches his beard, it indicates he is worried and tensed up about some problem.

Something as natural as clearing one's throat is indicative of the kind of person you are. When a person begins to address an audience, it is natural to clear the throat before speaking. This is a sign of tension. It indicates a nervous person. He is biding time before starting. More men than women use this technique. Children never show their nervousness this way.

The conscious throat-clearing sound made by an authoritative person, however, is a signal of being in control. It is a warning that whatever is being done must be stopped. Sometimes, a person clears the throat before asking a question. This is to attract attention and muster courage before asking the question.

The mother-child relationship is so close that a mother learns to read the body language of her child very quickly. Mothers instinctively know what their children think, feel, act or respond to. One of the earliest gestures a mother recognises is when her child is hiding or lying about something. When the child avoids looking at the mother, she is certain that the child is hiding something.

Even if the child is unable to speak, the mother comes to know about the child's needs by reading the body language. The mother can also sense when her child needs sleep. The child will become less active or get irritated.

The other gestures that are a quick give-away include blinking, looking at one's feet, shrugging the shoulders, swallowing repeatedly, wetting the lips, clearing the throat, rubbing the nose, scratching the head, rubbing the back of the neck and slouching.

As you set out to improve your personal image through better etiquette and manners in everyday life, you can further appreciate how people react. Once you understand their body reactions, be it at home, at work, or in society, it becomes easier to react to conversations in every situation. As people grow and begin to understand body language, they consciously learn to control themselves and prefer to communicate through words rather than by body signals. Educated and experienced persons learn to control their body language.

A progressive person cannot afford to be many persons in one. You would not like to be one either. Understand yourself. Adopt good etiquette and manners. Become the person you want to be.

❑ ❑ ❑

4

The Four Magic Words

"Politeness is like an air cushion; there may be nothing in it, but it eases our jolts wonderfully."

– Johnson

When Ali Baba used the magic words, "Open Sesame", it opened the door of a cave in the mountains where 40 thieves had hidden huge wealth in the form of gold, diamonds and precious stones. This enormous wealth turned him into a rich person and made his life easy.

In today's context, we have four magic words which can help in getting our work done quickly, making life much easier.

The first word is **PLEASE**. It rhymes with 'grease' and acts in much the same manner. While applying grease makes a machine run smoothly, affixing 'please' to any request or even a command helps in getting the work done quickly. Just saying 'please' softens the attitude of the other person towards you. I have used it many times with my family to get things done, even when they were unwilling to do the job in the first place.

The second word is **THANK YOU**. This word is not very popular in our country, as we feel it is our birthright to get things done by other people. Sometimes, we feel it is unnecessary or beneath our dignity to say these words to a waiter bringing a glass of water or a doorman outside a restaurant or shop, who are bound to do their duty anyway.

But saying these words makes a lot of difference. It never fails to bring a smile or an affirmative nod on the face of the other person. He feels his work, however unimportant it may seem, is noticed and appreciated.

The third word is **SORRY**. The words "I'm sorry" do not come easily out of our mouth. Every person has an ego, and these words, whenever uttered, tend to dent the ego. Again, we feel it is below our dignity to say sorry, even if we are at fault. But if we give it a good thought, we will realise that the word acts as a problem solver. Whether it is a hurt family member, an upset relative or an angry boss, this word acts as a soothing balm and helps smooth ruffled feathers.

Initially, it may seem painful to say this word. However, we should realise that accepting our mistake before others is a sign of strength, not weakness. But this word should be used only when we mean it and not as a means to escape anger or punishment. If we are really sorry, we should ensure that the mistake is never repeated. Repeating the mistake and saying 'Sorry' again and again only makes the word lose its magic.

The fourth magic word is **EXCUSE ME**. This is a polite word, used particularly to clear one's path, when there is restricted space and there are too many people in the way. Sometimes we use it to draw attention to ourselves in a gathering, be it a classroom, a conference room, seminar or any other type of public gathering. Even when two people are talking, this word can be used to interrupt the conversation. It is also used when one sneezes in the presence of others.

All these magic words can be made more effective when used with a smile and a pleasant tone of voice. If we consciously use these words in our daily life, it will certainly make a big difference. Things will get done faster, in a better manner, whether at home, in the office or amongst friends.

By making other people feel better, we ourselves feel better. So just use these words and see how they work like magic.

❏ ❏ ❏

5

Etiquette of Greeting People

It is customary to greet people when you meet them. Some say, "Good morning", or "Hello", others "Namaste" or "Namaskar". Some prefer, "Ram Ramji" or "Jai Sri Krishna". Sikhs say, "Sat Sri Akal". Muslims say, "Adabarz" or "Salaam Walaikum". Whatever the form of greeting, it immediately dissolves barriers between two persons and creates a feeling of oneness.

While greeting, some shake hands. Others join hands to say, "Namaskar". Some wave to say "Hi!". Others embrace. A few kiss on the cheek.

It is not possible to meet people who live away from us. Many of us are shy of writing letters. A few get tongue-tied expressing their feelings on phone. Relax! Greeting card manufacturers have made things easier for everyone. Different kinds of cards are available to convey sentiments appropriately. Be it different new years, festivals, birthdays and anniversaries, or Valentine's Day, Mother's Day, Father's Day and the like, there are cards to convey specific sentiments.

Those who greet others amiably find it easier to get along with people in daily life. Greetings motivate, inspire and get a conversation going. Greetings foster friendship. Learn the art of greeting people wherever you go. You will be welcome everywhere. And when you receive greetings, do not forget to send a "thank you" card.

❏ ❏ ❏

6

Use Me,
Don't Abuse Me

All material things in today's world are meant to provide comfort for human beings. Quite often, their presence is ignored and the very purpose forgotten. For instance, watches of all makes – even in gold, silver and diamonds – are available in today's market. But these are used more like pieces of jewellery, rather than utilities to keep track of time.

Decades ago, not many people had watches, but they really knew the value of time. They could tell the time simply by looking at the position of the sun. Today, people do not realise the importance of time. We can see students rushing to school to be in time for their classes, people running on the roads to catch a bus and passengers on the platform scrambling with their luggage to board the train. Even matters that need to be attended right away are postponed to a future date. Punctuality is one word that has largely been forgotten today.

The civic authorities provide dustbins to dispose of garbage. Do we use them? It is far easier to throw it across the street, or across the neighbour's boundary wall. We then wonder why so many flies and mosquitoes are hovering around!

Spittoons have been provided at many public places for *paan*-eaters to spit into. But ask any *paan*-eater and he will tell you there is more of a thrill spitting on walls and roads.

Why ignore the dustbin? Use it.

Historical monuments and buildings should be viewed and appreciated. Instead, many people write obscene words, scrawl romantic messages or even carve their initials on the walls. The graffiti on these walls would make anybody blush in shame and embarrassment.

At such places, people also leave behind food wrappers, plastic glasses, foodstuff, tins, bottles and other sundry items, littering the premises without a thought. We should refrain from such actions and throw all leftovers into dustbins provided by the civic authorities Some people make the lame excuse that there was no dustbin within sight. In this case, the simple solution would be to keep all the refuse in a polythene and take it with us. When we locate a dustbin later, we can then throw the polythene into it.

At home, the poor doormat comes in many varieties and sizes. It patiently waits for people to clean the underside of their shoes. But no, a little mud will not hurt the floor, we reason. The floor has to be mopped in the morning anyway.

Smoking is injurious to health. Ask the poor carpet, or the bed linen. Bearing the burns and the ash is the worst thing for them. The poor ashtrays also feel ignored. Nobody likes to use them.

The poor soap dish, the hand towels and taps are in no less trouble. The soap dish is ignored and the soap lies soggy. The towels are messy. The taps are left running. So what if there is water shortage? Can't a person be comfortable in his own home?

Everyone loves music. Different music systems are on sale in the market. Nobody wants to be left behind. Why should the neighbourhood not know that you have nothing short of a 1,000-watt system? So what if there are elderly and sick people around? If they find it disturbing, it is their problem! After all, you are playing the music system in your own home.

The next time you are organising a *jagrata*, or a birthday party, get the best loudspeaker system. After all, these functions are not celebrated everyday. If the system is not loud enough, how will the neighbourhood know you are celebrating!!

People build walls around their homes to keep intruders out. Walls provide an excellent place to stick posters of all descriptions. Big walls provide a nice place to paint messages on. Even the "No Parking" boards or private boards provide an ideal place to paste the smaller posters.

Each day, every one of us is trying the patience of our family members, friends, neighbours and others by doing things that can be avoided. Are we really so important that we do not need the goodwill of others? Are we really so helpless that on the pretext of personal comfort and pleasure we disturb and offend others?

A little thoughtfulness on our part can make the community a happier place to live in. Good etiquette and manners take one a long way towards building good relationships.

7

Standing in Queues

Queues are a part of modern life. It does not matter where you go, you will have to wait for your turn. We see queues everywhere. At the bus stop, the railway station, and at the airport. There are queues at the ration shop, the movie hall, and even at the self-service general store where we must wait our turn to pay for our purchases. We are not spared even in some restaurants. Register your name, and wait in the queue.

Human nature being what it is, people tend to get impatient with waiting. Some try to jump the queue. Others fret and fume. Some shout at the person in-charge. We feel embarrassed to be standing in a queue. We feel hurt that we have been made to wait.

An important consideration is whether it can be helped. Is there an alternative to this system? Is it not fair that each is served on a first-come-first-served basis? The fault is not with the system. The fault is with an individual's attitude. Why should one feel embarrassed standing in a queue? If one were not to disturb or shout at the person in-charge, the service would be faster. Everyone would be attended to. There would be more satisfaction.

The next time you feel upset standing in a queue, ask yourself why you did not feel the same way while waiting for a table in a restaurant. Obviously because you were looking forward to a sumptuous meal! When you wait in a queue, you are waiting for a special service. If it weren't urgent, you would not have been there.

Standing in queues also demands we respect the elderly and the disabled. We can easily accommodate them in the queue and treat them with due respect.

Accept queues as a part of modern life. Do not be impatient. Do not jump queues. Wait for your turn. Extend courtesy and respect to everyone. You will get these back. Good etiquette and manners never fail.

8

Smoking Etiquette

All cigarette packets carry a statutory warning: *Smoking is injurious to health*. Despite this warning, if people wish to smoke, it is their personal decision. However, it does not give them the licence to discomfort or put those who do not smoke at risk.

Smoking is prohibited at many public places like airports and railway stations, cinema halls and theatres, in hospitals, libraries and several other places. It is also prohibited in public conveyances like trains and buses. Many business houses also prohibit smoking in their premises. There are specific reasons for these restrictions. All smokers must observe them.

Smoking in a no-smoking zone. Is it right?

If you are uncertain whether smoking is permitted in a particular place, seek permission from the available individual, asking him if smoking there is permitted. Even where smoking is permitted, it is basic courtesy to seek the permission of those accompanying you if it is all right to smoke. Unknown to you, a person could be allergic to smoke. Elderly persons are particularly sensitive to this problem.

Research on smoking has revealed that it is not only the smoker who is adversely affected by the cigarette smoke, but people around him are also affected. These passive smokers are equally at risk to smoke-related ailments. Therefore, one should be particularly careful not to smoke before children and elders, as they are more prone to cough and other related problems. Moreover, it is disrespectful to smoke in the presence of elders. Smoking in the presence of children also sets a wrong example, since they might get the impression that there is nothing wrong with smoking.

When you smoke, ensure that it does not disturb others. Use an ashtray. After you have stopped smoking, put out the stub. Do not throw cigarette butts on the floor. Even when you throw a cigarette stub on the roadside, crumple it with your foot. Many a serious fire has been ignited with a cigarette butt thrown carelessly.

Your home may be your domain, but don't forget your family lives there too. Don't let your wife have to constantly complain about the ash thrown on the carpet or the upholstery. She will be sore about the butts scattered all around the house, and about the burnt bed linen. And do remember that those who smoke cannot expect their children not to smoke.

❏ ❏ ❏

27

9

Drinking Etiquette

*"The first draught serveth for health, the second for pleasure,
the third for shame, and the fourth for madness."*

– Anacharsis

Whatever we may feel about it, drinking is on the increase, both amongst the young and the old. Ladies are not far behind. It is becoming fashionable to host cocktail parties where liquor and snacks are served.

Some carry their liquor well. Drinking makes them happy. A few make a fool of themselves. They drink beyond their limit and end up making a nuisance of themselves for the host.

How is it that some people can drink a lot and still remain sober, while others get tipsy even with small quantities? To appreciate this, one needs to understand that alcohol is an intoxicating drug. Its wide-scale use makes us believe that it is not. Doctors confirm that in small quantities alcohol can be beneficial in keeping one healthy. However, just like with other drugs, sensitivity to alcohol varies from one person to another. One cannot assert what quantity would be right for anyone. Everyone needs to discover this themselves.

People either drink beer that comes ready to serve after chilling, or whisky, vodka, gin or rum, with or without water or soda. Some prefer brandy or liqueur after dinner. Wines that come ready to serve in different varieties, like white or red wines, are also becoming popular. Champagne is served on special occasions. A variety of tasty snacks are served with drinks. The two combine well with each other.

The British, who brought sophistication into drinking, use different kinds of glasses to serve drinks. Whereas beer is served in mugs, or large glasses, whisky is served in smaller straight glasses. Wine and champagne are served in round glasses. Brandy and liqueurs are served in still smaller glasses.

Drinking etiquette requires that one should not create any kind of unpleasantness for hosts and companions. To ensure this, one should drink in moderation. Unlike food that is digested and absorbed in the intestines, alcohol is absorbed in the stomach. Drink slowly, sipping the drink rather than gulping it. Salted snacks aid this process. Do not mix drinks. Sometimes they can have a bad effect. If you drink, do not use sleeping drugs. Alcohol and sleeping drugs form a bad combination.

Alcohol initially stimulates a person. As the quantity of alcohol increases in the blood, depression sets in. This can result in a hangover the next morning. Drinking more is not a cure for hangover. Drink coffee instead.

More ladies are drinking today than ever before. If they were to keep within limits, it is fine. Again, since it is difficult to define the right limit, excesses are possible. Drunkenness in women can be interpreted wrongly. It also gives rise to other issues. Therefore, it is necessary that women should maintain moderation if they drink.

When you feel you have had enough, call it a day. Do not let anybody force you into having another drink. "One for the road" is a folly. You are drinking for pleasure. Do not let it become displeasure – for you and others!

❑ ❑ ❑

10

Tipping Etiquette

One needs to tip for many services and wonders what an appropriate tip would be under certain circumstances. It is uncommon to tip shop assistants. However, if a shop assistant helps you carry packages into your car, particularly when it is parked far away, it may be all right to tip him. In India, tipping taxi drivers is also not common. But it would be appropriate to tip him if he has been especially courteous and helpful in reaching your destination.

In all good restaurants the waiters expect a tip. Ten per cent of the bill is a fair amount. If the bill is low, you can tip a little more. If the bill is high, you can reduce the tip somewhat. In some restaurants, a service charge is included in the bill. Despite this, the waiters do expect a tip. If in doubt, you can always ask the manager.

Most hotels include service charges and other expenses in the bill. It is not necessary to tip in these places. But if you receive special attention from a staff member, you can give an appropriate tip. In hotels where no service charges are included in the bills and you have stayed there for a day or more, you can tip the staff suitably, passing the tips individually to the dining room staff, room attendants, housekeeping staff and bellboys.

There will be other occasions like festivals when domestic staff, the postman, municipal staff and others expect tips. You can tip them depending upon the kind of service they provide and the custom of tipping in the locality.

11

Etiquette of Making Complaints

Everyone needs to make complaints sometimes. We may be aggrieved about poor service, the quality of a product, or feel let down because of a written or verbal contract that has been breached.

Whenever a person is aggrieved, the immediate reaction is a feeling of being cheated or taken for a ride. In such situations, one tends to lose one's temper and ends up being rude or even uncouth, while lodging a protest or complaint. This can sometimes be counterproductive and rather than gaining redressal, it may only exacerbate the problem.

Good etiquette requires all complaints be made in a civil manner. The complaint must also be lodged with the right authority. In a restaurant, if the waiter cannot resolve your complaint, speak to the steward or the person in-charge at the counter. In a hotel, if room service cannot resolve your complaint, speak to the reception. If still unsatisfied, talk to the manager. You will get results.

If you have a complaint against an auto-rickshaw or taxi driver, report it to the person in-charge at the stand. If necessary, complain to the traffic police. When travelling by rail, report your complaint to the attendant, the train ticket examiner or the train superintendent. If still aggrieved, speak to the station superintendent or report the matter to the General Manager at the regional headquarters of the Railways.

Sometimes we receive goods of an inferior quality or find the after-sales service is bad. Lodge a complaint with the dealer who sold you the item. In case no proper response is forthcoming, contact the manufacturer's service division. If still unsatisfied, write to the company's General Manager. If all this fails, contact the local Consumer Forum. If necessary, file a suit. It costs nothing. Nor do you need a lawyer. You can represent yourself.

Many refuse to complain because it implies time and effort. But if you seek value for money, do assert your rights. Lodging genuine complaints improves service for everyone. Good etiquette ensures happiness for all.

❑ ❑ ❑

12

Borrowing and Lending Etiquette

In one of his plays, Shakespeare said, *"Neither a borrower nor a lender be; a loan oft loses both itself and a friend."* This is true even today, as it was when first written. We see it happening everyday. Those who cannot resist borrowing will continue to ask. People are hesitant to lend. Those that are shy to refuse give in, hoping that they will get back what they have lent.

Good etiquette requires that one must be self-sufficient and not borrow. Even if one must borrow, good manners require that promises be honoured. Whatever has been borrowed must be returned with gratitude and a smile.

One should avoid borrowing money. This can be the cause of many a misunderstanding. If one is compelled to borrow due to unforeseen circumstances, one must return the money when promised, or preferably earlier. At the time of repayment, it is good manners to offer interest on the money, even if you have taken it from a friend. Nobody keeps his money idle. Even in the bank it earns interest. If the friend refuses to accept interest, express your gratitude in clear terms. The friend must know that his magnanimity has been appreciated.

Borrowing of personal belongings like clothes, shoes, and toiletries like nail polish or lipstick is not a good habit. Except between brothers and sisters, it must not be done. Similarly, most people do not appreciate the borrowing of household items such as music systems, or provisions like tea and sugar, or other items. Many people borrow books and magazines, and then just forget about returning these. They may feel that perhaps the lender has forgotten these. It is never so. The lender feels cheated, and can never forget it. On occasions, the lender will talk about it, tarnishing the image of the borrower.

13

Using Loudspeakers

"Manners easily and rapidly mature into morals."

– H. Mann

One of the many nuisances of modern life is the excessive use of loudspeakers. When the loudspeaker was invented, the purpose was to enable people sitting at the far end of the gathering to hear the speaker clearly. We have now carried this use to the extreme. We have loudspeakers in temples, mosques, marriage parties, fetes, and other religious and non-religious gatherings.

In cities, noise pollution has reached alarming proportions, leading to problems like insomnia and deafness. Have we realised that this could be disturbing a large number of children who may be studying for their exams? Have we ever given a thought that the noise could be disturbing the elderly and the sick, who may be seeking rest? Few inventions have been as misused as the loudspeaker.

In many cities the police have imposed restrictions on the use of loudspeakers, restricting these to certain hours. But many people circumvent the rules and find ways to misuse loudspeakers. Make sure that you are not one of them. If you need to use a loudspeaker, tune it so that only the audience within the premises can hear it. Under no circumstances should the loudspeaker horn be fitted outside the building for the neighbourhood to hear. It is your programme. Please restrict it to yourself and your audience. The neighbourhood will appreciate your good etiquette.

❑ ❑ ❑

Telephone Etiquette

Perhaps nothing has brought people closer across cities, countries and continents as the telephone has. Today, one can talk to people even in remote corners of the world. Earlier, not every home was fortunate enough to have a telephone. Now we have small personal exchange systems even in homes. These connect every room to the outside world. Business houses have a telephone on every desk.

Telephones have even gone to remote villages. Where individuals cannot afford them, there are public call offices spread all over the country. One can talk to any part of the world from these booths.

*Be considerate to others in the queue –
keep your conversation short.*

Besides being able to talk, telephones have made it possible to send documents through fax machines connected to the telephone line. Documents can now be sent within minutes. The Internet connected through the telephone has brought the world to every home. You can send messages and pictures, and even chat with people around the world. Through the Internet, a vast storehouse of knowledge is available to you at home.

All these developments have given rise to the need for good manners on the telephone. To begin with, understand how a telephone works. Besides the number keys ranging from 0 to 9, there are other keys like mute, pause, flash and redial. Read the telephone booklet. Many telephone instruments have the facility to store telephone numbers. You can key these numbers into the instrument, and on pressing a single button the number is dialled automatically. Similarly, on pressing the redial button, the last number you dialled will be repeated.

Every telephone user has a number. The first part of this number refers to the number of the telephone exchange, and the rest to the user. For example, if your number is 2722 1234, the exchange number is 2722, and your number is 1234. Every city has a number too. For example, Delhi is 011, Mumbai is 022, Kolkata is 033 and Chennai is 044. A number also identifies every country. The number 91 identifies India.

It is not practical to remember the numbers of all the persons one needs to contact. The telephone department supplies a directory of the local telephone numbers to all users. Some organisations have supplemented this service by publishing special directories referred to as *Yellow Pages*, as these are printed on yellow paper. For daily use it is not possible to keep referring to these directories. Therefore, one must maintain a personal telephone directory where one can note down the numbers of persons one speaks to frequently. For emergency use, the numbers of the hospital, fire brigade, railways, the bus terminal, police station and the family doctor may be noted on the first page.

When making official calls, you must be clear about the person you wish to speak to, and what you want to convey. This will ensure no time or money is wasted on wrong calls. Furthermore, whenever you dial a number make sure it is the right number.

When you make an official or business call and the person you wish to speak with is not available, leave your contact details with the receptionist or telephone operator. This will ensure that when the person gets back, s/he will know that you had called and would be in a position to call back if they so desire.

When you need to dial a number from a place where a personal exchange is installed, as in some homes or in offices and hotels, you first need to dial a number like '0' or '9', or some other pre-set number, to get the dial tone. In hotels, this number is noted in the directory of services provided in every room.

In some cases, as at railway stations or airports, you may be put on to a number that is connected to a computer. When you are connected to the railway station, this number will automatically give instructions. It may ask you whether you want to inquire about departures, or arrivals. It will also direct you to key in a particular number for departures, and another one for arrivals. When you follow instructions, you may now be asked the train number. When you key in the train number, you will get a response saying, "The train is running 45 minutes late." This way you can get information about many services conveniently on the telephone.

In many cities you can get personal services like food or groceries by using the telephone. When you ask for home delivery, identify yourself clearly and give your precise address and the telephone number you are speaking from. To ensure it is not a hoax call, the service provider may ring back immediately to reconfirm the order.

When dialling international numbers, it is good manners to check the time of the country where you are calling. It may be daytime here, but it could well be midnight in the country where you wish to call and you might disturb the recipient at an odd hour.

When you speak on the phone, it is your voice that makes or mars your image. It is, therefore, important that you speak courteously on the phone. Be polite. Answer the call gently. Do not use improper language. While on the phone, do not converse with others at your end. Telephone instruments are very sensitive and pick up voices from a distance. Sometimes it can create misunderstandings. In case you get a wrong number, simply say "sorry" and gently put the receiver down.

A receptionist must always be courteous
to create a good image of the organisation.

Receptionists at business houses need to be particularly careful about voice training. Their job depends upon it. When you speak on the phone, let it reflect a smiling face. Let there be an air of helpfulness in your tone. Politeness and courtesy reflect good etiquette. Your image will linger in the minds of people you talk to on the telephone.

❏ ❏ ❏

15

Mobile Phone Etiquette

With almost all cities being linked through mobile phones, the number of users has grown dramatically. With cheaper and better services, and the availability of cheaper handsets, every home will soon avail of the services. With this has arisen the need for good manners and etiquette when using mobile phones.

Many people use mobile phones not because they need to, but because it is perceived to be a status symbol. Youngsters are particularly guilty on this count. It may be all right to carry a mobile phone when travelling, or when one needs to stay away from home until late into the night. But it is certainly not something to carry to school or college.

A user subscribes to the cellular phone service for personal convenience. If you wish to talk to the person, it is simple courtesy to first try and get the person on the landline. Only if the person is unavailable on the landline, and you need to get in touch quickly, should you dial the mobile number.

Many mobile phone users are guilty of keeping their instruments on at restaurants, cinema halls and temples, during meetings and at places where these can disturb others. Daily, we hear mobile phones ringing in the wrong places. It is good manners to keep the ringer off when you are in a public place where it can disturb people. Use the vibration mode instead. Many mobile services offer a facility where they can transfer messages left for you. Some service providers also offer the service of informing you about the numbers that called when your phone was switched off.

If you need to respond to calls made when you are in a public place, remember that speaking even in hushed tones can disturb others. Excuse yourself, and go to a place where you can speak without disturbing others. A mobile is useful when you are travelling by a vehicle. You can be traced in case of an emergency or make a call if the need arises.

However, it is dangerous and against the law to use mobiles while driving. Many accidents have occurred simply because the driver's attention had been distracted by a call. If you need to take or make an urgent call, stop the car by the roadside and then speak. It could mean the difference between life and death.

Etiquette at Home

Do you live in a house or a home? The two words may be synonyms, but there is a difference between the two. A house is a structure of bricks, mortar and wood, which may be fully furnished but devoid of your personal touch. Although you live here, it is not a place that you can call your own, perhaps because it is rented.

Whereas a home is not just a place where you live, but where you have invested your time, energy and feelings. It is the finer feelings and emotions of the people who live in it that contribute to making the precincts a home. It does not matter whether this structure is a hut, a flat, a bungalow, or a palace.

Learning etiquette should begin in childhood.

Happiness in the home comes from a definite discipline accepted by householders. It comes from cordial relations, good etiquette and manners observed by everyone.

Ideally, the day should begin with greeting each other. Some may say, "Good morning". Others prefer "Namaskar" or "Namaste". Greeting each other is a sure way to express your interest in the welfare of the others.

The bathroom is the next place to be in. In all good homes, etiquette requires that everyone should use the bathroom, not monopolise it. After use, leave it clean and dry. If there are clothes to be washed, place them properly. Do not throw them around to be trampled upon. A good rule is to leave the bathroom in a shape you would like it to be when you need to use it.

Families that work like a team are happy families. Everyone shares the work and responsibilities. In some homes, it is customary to eat together at the table. Sometimes, it is not possible as children go to school at different times, the man of the house has to go to work, and others may have their own routine. Still, it is good etiquette if the whole family has dinner together.

Food must be eaten with the mouth closed. Chew food quietly. It is ungracious to smack lips, or to chew with the mouth open. Some like to eat and talk at the same time. This should be avoided, as there is the likelihood of food particles or spittle being thrown onto someone, or into another's plate. Food on the table is for everyone to share. It is not good manners to overfill the plate. Serve yourself as much as you need. A second helping can always be taken. One should take as much as one can eat, and not leave it on the plate.

Children imitate elders and slowly but surely pick up habits that they see. They should be taught to differentiate between good and bad habits. Teach them to use the four magic words with a smile. Teach them to respect their elders and teachers. They must speak to elders without raising their

Food on the table is for everyone to share.

voice if they disagree, putting across their point of view patiently. At home, they should abide by the etiquette adopted by elders. The television is for everyone to watch. Loud music should not be played when others are resting. Shouting, screaming and throwing tantrums must be avoided.

Children must eat meals with everyone else, not when they choose to. They must help in the household work. Being cordial and polite can take one a long way in life. They must be responsible for looking after their things and keeping their room clean.

Parents and grandparents should appreciate the problems of growing up. These can be difficult years for the children. They should not compare their children with others or unduly praise other children.

A home is where the heart is. The heart is happy where one lives in dignity. Happiness comes with care, courtesy, respect and thoughtfulness for each other. Etiquette and good manners considerably reduce friction in close relationships. One then learns to face the outside world with courage and confidence.

❏ ❏ ❏

17

Dress Etiquette

One should dress as well as one can afford to. Your clothes speak loudly about your tastes, disposition, likes and dislikes. Clothes help draw immediate attention. Besides protecting one from the weather, like personal charm, clothes must delight the eye and the mind. Dress to suit the occasion. Clothes must be comfortable to wear, easy to care for, and elegant to look at.

At home one can dress casually. During holidays one can dress in shorts and T-shirts, or as one pleases.

An office is a working place. Clothes should not be a cause of distraction. In an office, dress conservatively. Men are best in a shirt and trousers. Neckties are optional in some offices. In winters, woollen sweaters and pullovers should be sober, never bright and gaudy. Lady employees too need to dress conservatively in office. Salwar-kameez and sari are ideal. If used to wearing slacks, the tops must be long. Avoid low necklines or backless blouses. Jewellery should be restricted to the minimum, say, small earrings and a ring. A chain is optional. But nothing should be loud. Avoid heavy makeup and strong perfumes.

When attending formal functions at the office or socially, dress formally. Men can wear suits complete with necktie. Ladies can wear heavier saris and salwar-kameez for formal occasions, and jewellery to match.

Footwear is equally important. So are the accessories like handbags for ladies, particularly on formal occasions. Ensure these match well.

For a funeral or condolence ceremony, it is customary to wear white, or light pastel shades. Avoid reds, maroons, pinks and dark colours.

At all other times, clothes must be attractive, not garish.

❑ ❑ ❑

18

Etiquette with Children

Everyone loves children. They are an extension of our lives, a mirror of our hopes, aspirations and dreams. However, it does not mean that we do not need to discipline them, or teach them etiquette and good manners.

Everyday we notice how these loving kids create a ruckus when we visit the neighbours or friends. They will pick flowers in the garden, run about the house toppling things, and walk on the carpet with muddy feet. When they eat, they will put the plate on the sofa upholstery. When they visit the toilet, they mess it up. They do not realise that their actions may offend the hosts. As parents, it is your responsibility to make the kids behave themselves, particularly when they are in somebody else's house.

Children grow up with the habits you teach them. If you teach them to be clean, careful and considerate, they will be the same in their adult life. But if you let them do as they please, do not be surprised when they become irresponsible adults. Learn to differentiate between discipline and suppression. Discipline is positive. It encourages self-control. Suppression is negative. It blocks the expression of individuality.

Habits adopted in the first seven years of life last a lifetime. Teach your children good manners. Teach them to differentiate between good and bad. Teach them to be happy. Well-mannered children are sheer joy – and welcome everywhere.

❏ ❏ ❏

Dating Etiquette
for Youngsters

With more co-educational schools and colleges, and greater opportunities for youngsters to interact with each other, dating is now a part of daily life not only in metro cities, but also in smaller towns. Since dating involves a meeting of opposite sexes, several questions perturb both the boy and the girl.

Young men worry about their clothes, manners and habits. Young ladies are anxious about their clothes, and also how attractive they appear. Both may be tongue-tied, anxious and uneasy. The best rule is to relax. You have nothing to lose. Be your natural self. The purpose of dating is to interact with the opposite sex. It is only a stepping-stone to adult relationships.

Where should the couple go together? Some like to go to a nearby park, a garden, or a picnic spot. Others may prefer to go for a movie or a play, followed by some refreshments. Some may like to visit a discotheque or a pub. Many prefer to spend the evening together at home, sharing common interests like books, stamps, coins, or even listening to their favourite music. The important thing is that both must enjoy being together.

Many urban youngsters have their own vehicle. If one is not available, the couple need not waste money hiring a taxi. Do not show off. If both partners are from the same background, they should keep within their means. Use public transport. Do not let secondary issues spoil your fun.

Who should spend money on a date? Some girls expect that since they have been invited out, it is the responsibility of the young man to pay. Many young men are willing to do so. However, most ladies are fair about it. They appreciate that their companions have limited means and offer to go Dutch, each paying one's share.

Should they exchange gifts and presents? It is not necessary to give a gift unless the occasion requires it. Giving and receiving gifts is a two-way gesture. It is important that the value of the gift should not cause undue embarrassment to either person. The value of the gift does not matter. It is the sentiments behind the gift that count.

Late nights do not bother youngsters as much as it bothers parents. This should be avoided. Besides, parents must be informed with whom the youngster is going and where. When are they likely to get back? If you get late on a date, it is proper to inform your parents on phone. If it gets late, good manners require that the lady must be escorted home.

Amongst the many temptations that new-found independence offers, there is also the temptation of experimenting with smoking, drinking, drugs and sex. Many youngsters do not see any harm in experimenting with them. But youngsters must remember that it is easier to control oneself the first time a temptation comes their way. It becomes difficult the second time around. If vices were acceptable in daily life, nobody would have objected to them.

Should young people hold hands, kiss, or become intimate? To understand this, young people need to understand that emotionally men and women are different. They interpret each other's actions differently. Certain moral standards have been bred into us through customs and conventions. Let us respect them in our own interests. Dating is intended to provide companionship with the opposite sex. That is all one should look forward to.

20

Etiquette for Ladies

Good etiquette and manners are for all to follow. There are some that are peculiar to ladies. These need their special attention. Ladies' kitty parties and coffee get-togethers have become popular in larger cities, as well as in smaller towns. Even in rural areas, it is not unusual for ladies to get together and discuss matters of mutual interest. These get-togethers offer good relief from the monotony of daily life and ladies find it emotionally invigorating.

What needs to be guarded against is that these get-togethers do not degenerate into gossip sessions or eating parties. Such activities do one no good. Indulging in gossip is a sure way of creating misunderstandings, losing friends, and winning enemies. When you hear gossip, don't pass it on. Ignore it.

Is it proper for women to smoke and drink? Smoking and drinking by women is on the increase. One reason for this is that everyone else is doing it. Others drink for the temporary pleasure it provides. Nothing can be said in favour of drinking by women. Alcohol weakens the reflexes. It is habit forming. It makes one vulnerable to accidents and sickness.

Many women begin smoking to taste the forbidden. Once tried, they find it difficult to quit. Tobacco is addictive. It is also dangerous for health. Furthermore, it is unsightly to see women smoke and it sets a bad example for children. Good etiquette and manners require that women set the right example for their children.

❏ ❏ ❏

21

Etiquette with Domestic Help

Everybody desires the convenience of domestic help. Some hire part-time help. Others have full-time workers. Both have some problems. Domestic workers are human beings. They have their own hopes and aspirations. They work out of necessity. Since many people consider domestic work menial in comparison to other vocations, the self-esteem of the worker is always under pressure. To ease this pressure, the ideal relationship is to treat domestic help as part of the family. Some people do so and realise its benefits.

However, problems arise when a member of the family expects more from the domestic worker than is reasonable, or the worker refuses to do what is legitimately his responsibility. To ease the situation, it is best to clearly define the responsibilities. Let all the family members know about it. Nobody should cross the limits of fair understanding.

Strictly observe the working time. If there is need for deviation occasionally, this must be through mutual understanding. Pay workers on time. Nothing provokes a worker more than not being paid on time. There must be clear understanding about rest and leave. Occasionally, the domestic help does expect tips and gifts on occasions like Diwali and other festivals.

Never use foul language with domestic help. Workers should also never reply back or act cheeky. It should be a fair relationship on either side. Just as the worker can leave if not happy working for a home, you have the liberty to relieve the worker if unsatisfied.

Do not try to act tough with domestic help. Some of them can be aggressive and unsavoury. Ladies, children and elderly people are particularly vulnerable. Always check their antecedents with past employers. And have your domestic help's name registered with the local police by using diplomatic means. A photograph can also be left along with details like full name and local and native address.

❏ ❏ ❏

22

Party Etiquette

Sometimes you may want to invite friends, or maybe even the boss and colleagues, for a meal. A party is an occasion to make the invitees feel welcome, a time to be happy together.

To ensure a successful party, an occasion that everyone will remember, plan ahead. Good food is important, but that is not all. Make the party interesting. Decorate the table. Do not overdo it with flowers or decorations that would make movement of dishes difficult. In the daytime, use a gay tablecloth and napkins. For formal or semi-formal parties, white is still the most popular choice. Alternatively, you could try pastel shades.

Make your party enjoyable for everyone.

Most homes now use plates. Even if it is a formal occasion, and you are serving Indian food, it will be all right to lay the table in the western style. To lay the table, place a side plate, a large plate for the main dishes, a fork on the left side and a knife (optional) on the right side of the main plate, and a tablespoon along with a dessertspoon above the plate. The glass for water can be placed on the right top hand side just touching the tip of the knife. You can place the napkin on the side plate, or in a glass. If soup is to be served, the main plate may be placed after the soup is over. In that case you will need to place a soupspoon on the right of the knife.

If it is to be a very formal affair, and many courses are to be served, you will need enough trained staff to change the large plate after every course. Generally this is not done because of practical problems involved. One main plate is placed for each person. The dessert plate is placed after the meal is over and the main plate has been removed.

You will do well to have everything ready before the guests arrive. You can put the food in the service dishes and place them in a hot case. *Chapattis* stay warm and soft if placed in a clean napkin kept in a closed dish. This way you can attend to the guests personally, and place the food on the table when required.

When you have done everything in advance, it will allow you a little time to relax, dress up, and check the final arrangements before the guests arrive. When the guests arrive, receive them personally. Offer them seats as planned. Serve drinks and snacks. As the guests arrive, introduce them to each other. This way they can be comfortable and converse with each other. Put friends with similar interests together. Get a conversation going and then excuse yourself to meet other guests.

If the music is on, play it softly. It should not interfere with friends talking to each other. If there are party games, they must be arranged well in advance. Have somebody with natural leadership traits supervise them.

If the number of invitees is high, it may not be practical to have a sit-down meal. In that case you could have a buffet. The menu will then have to be planned to make it convenient to eat from a plate with a fork or spoon. Avoid too many dishes. Plan items that combine well. If there is soup, it can be served before the meal in cups.

If the party is for a special occasion, make it symbolic of the occasion – for instance, Diwali with lights and decorations. Children's parties can be made special with buntings, balloons, caps and decorative items.

If you are visiting a party as a guest, show your graciousness by acknowledging the invitation. Confirm the time, date and place. Confirm that you will attend. Reach at the appointed time. Appreciate the hospitality. Meet as many people as you can. Make new friends. If drinks are served, do not get drunk. Eat moderately. Do not overstay. When the party comes to a close, personally thank the host and hostess. Tell them you have enjoyed being together.

❏ ❏ ❏

23

Etiquette at Weddings

A marriage is always a great occasion for all family members and friends to meet. People travel great distances to be together. There is great interaction between family and friends. Most people are happy. Some are not. They are hurt because of some neglect of etiquette.

You could be part of a wedding as a host or a guest. Both need to observe special etiquette. As a host your first responsibility is to issue proper invitations. You will do well to make a list of relatives and friends whom you wish to invite for the wedding. Most people draw upon their personal telephone directory for preparing the invitee list. You may need to send personal letters to some relatives, particularly if they are living afar. They may need to make rail reservations and also ensure that their children's studies are not affected.

While drafting the invitation card, many people make the mistake of including names of some relatives who are close, and leave out others. This can cause resentment amongst those whose names are left out. When in doubt, avoid additional names altogether.

As a host when you invite guests, their stay is your responsibility. This is a difficult job, particularly when everyone seeks comfort and security as they may be carrying expensive clothes and jewellery. Since people have a tendency to compare, and interpret circumstances to suit their convenience, the question of accommodation for the guests needs special attention.

Lavishness in serving food is part of Indian hospitality. Do not let the guests feel that there is not enough, as some wastage is common on these occasions.

The timings of functions are yet another subject where differences of opinion prevail. Everyone has his own concept of time. Since people tend to break discipline, particularly with regard to time, others may grumble about the lack of punctuality.

A marriage is a special occasion. There is bound to be much gaiety, singing and dancing. You may enjoy it. Sometimes it can be a nuisance for others, particularly if you are living in a flat in a big building housing many families.

The wedding procession can be a source of much irritation and inconvenience to many when traffic is blocked and no attention is paid to honking vehicles. Do ensure all such irritants are kept to the minimum.

As a host, at the wedding reception you need to be the first to reach the venue and the last to leave. Ensure that the physical arrangements are all in place. The bride and groom must reach in time. Receive guests at the gate. Make them feel welcome. They must find their visit enjoyable. When they leave do not forget to say "thank you" for the time they have spared to grace the occasion.

As a host, the best rule is to maintain your cool at all times. It is your function. Everyone is your guest. If someone is hurt, apologise. Try to make everyone comfortable. Eventually, it is your courtesy and hospitality that will make the wedding memorable.

As a guest at a wedding, be gracious. Do not find faults. The hosts could be under much pressure. Not everyone can attend to everything. Meet and congratulate the couple, the parents and the relatives. It is customary to carry gifts at weddings. If it is an informal relationship, you can discuss what you would like to present at the wedding. This helps avoid duplication and wastage. When the relationship is formal, it is customary to give cash. Write your name legibly on the envelope. Hand over the envelope to the bride and groom or the parents, so that it reaches the right person.

Good etiquette and manners at a wedding keep everyone in a happy frame of mind, making it a truly memorable occasion.

❏ ❏ ❏

24

Etiquette with Pets

Pets are like children and give us great happiness. Although they are companions that do not speak, yet they give us unlimited love. Without them, we feel incomplete.

Like children, pets too need special care. They need to be kept clean, fed properly and taken out. When unwell, they need to be taken to the veterinarian.

Just as we may find our children lovable, and others may not, it is the same with pets. We may enjoy pets. Others may not. People may be irritated when dogs bark or cats mew. One may enjoy the chirping of birds or talking parrots, while others may find these irritating. Enjoy your pets. But do not impose them on others. When you take your dog out, use a leash. Ensure they do not dirty other people's gardens or premises. People living in apartments can be particularly sensitive about noisy pets, or dirty passages and entry to buildings. Make sure that your pets do not cause any inconvenience to other people.

The most popular pets are dogs. Some breeds like Alsatians, Labradors, Doberman Pinschers and Great Danes can be quite large in size, which arouses fear in many people, particularly children. It is better to keep such dogs in a separate room or leashed when guests arrive. When we take such dogs for walks, they must always be on leash so that it does not cause any inconvenience or fear amongst people.

Such pets need ample open space to keep them physically fit. If one intends to keep such pets, there should be ample open space, as in bungalows. Keeping such pets in cramped premises, such as a flat, is not good for their physical well-being.

Cleanliness of pets is very important. Dirty pets are not only a risk to themselves, but also to you and your children. Have them checked by a veterinarian periodically. If they need to be vaccinated, ensure that it is done in time. Pets are prohibited in certain places like restaurants, clubs, buses, etc. Please follow the rules. If you want to enjoy having pets, you will need to follow the etiquette of keeping pets.

❑ ❑ ❑

25

Commuting Etiquette

Everybody needs to commute to the place of work everyday. Some use their personal vehicles; others use shared vehicles, or the public transport system. Millions commute to work each morning. After a difficult day, they are again on the way home every evening. People can be in a bad mood. Tempers may be frayed and some people could be waiting to shout back. Etiquette and good manners inspire self-restraint.

Those with their own vehicles need to face the never-ending queues of vehicles moving in each direction. However, others face additional problems.

Some companies provide group pick-ups by special vehicles. This form of commuting is comfortable, as one is free from the hassles of driving and parking. The success of the system depends upon punctuality. You will need to be at the appointed pick-up point a few minutes before the scheduled arrival of the vehicle.

If you pool vehicles, each person taking his car to office once or twice every week, it will require commitment. For the system to work, everyone must understand personal responsibilities. Good etiquette does not permit excuses.

Those who do not need to go far can avail of auto-rickshaws or taxis. In that case, one needs to arrive at the nearest stand in time. Finding a suitable vehicle can be difficult in the evenings.

Those who use buses need to be well acquainted with bus numbers, their routes and timings. Bus stops are provided

Do not occupy seats reserved for ladies.

for shelter, but in inclement weather, one must make appropriate arrangements. In the interests of discipline, one needs to get accustomed to queues at bus stops. Rather than buy a ticket everyday, one needs to have a monthly pass. That saves one the inconvenience of carrying small change. At peak hours, the buses are rather full, and one will need to be careful about pickpockets. One will also need to get used to sitting and standing in moving buses. As in all things, courtesy and good manners help in making the journey hassle-free. During rush hours, get up at least one stop before your scheduled drop. You can then get off quickly at your stop.

A large number of people commute by local trains daily. They hold monthly passes. Since the stoppages of these trains are short, one has to be swift in getting into and off the train. There are special coaches for first class travel, and for ladies. It is not always possible to get seats at peak hours. Therefore, one will need to learn to travel standing. One will also have to be careful about pickpockets. To avoid problems, carry your pass safely. Do not eat anything given by unknown persons. Good manners will bring dividends.

❑ ❑ ❑

26

Etiquette on the Road

Roads connect people and places. A road is a public place for everyone to use. Therefore, besides pedestrians, one is bound to see vehicles of all description on the road. Some vehicles move slowly. Others move fast. The rule is, the slower vehicles move on the left side, and the faster ones on their right.

In the interests of discipline and public safety, many facilities have been devised. Roads may be divided with a road divider or a yellow line, and driving lanes may be painted. Traffic lights may be installed. Speed breakers may be provided. For the convenience of pedestrians, zebra crossings, overhead bridges, or underground tunnels may be provided. Take advantage of these provisions. They are not obstructions to your movement. They are conveniences devised for public safety.

It does not matter whether you are a pedestrian, or are driving a vehicle. The moment discipline on the road is ignored it becomes a dangerous place. The best safety device is a careful person. Be careful yourself. Teach carefulness to other members of your family.

As a pedestrian: You must walk cautiously on one side of the road. While crossing a road, first look to the right, and then to the left. Preferably cross at zebra crossings only. At night, be extra cautious. Wear light-coloured clothes. Sometimes, dark-coloured clothes are not visible in the light of a vehicle.

Roads are meant for people – not litter.

Occasionally, you might not feel like waiting for a bus or walking and decide to take the easy way out — taking a lift. You should never take this risk. People taking lifts, particularly women, have landed in unsavoury situations. You might be robbed, kidnapped, molested or raped. Avoid taking lifts at all costs.

As a driver: While driving a vehicle, never give lifts to strangers as you could also end up in unsavoury situations. In big cities particularly, it is definitely not safe to do so. There have been instances when call-girls have asked for lifts and then robbed the driver, threatening to scream if he did not hand over all valuables.

When driving a vehicle it is thoughtfulness for one another that helps maintain discipline on the road. Follow the rule of slower vehicles driving on the left, and faster ones on the right. Always give way to traffic on the right. As far as possible, avoid overtaking. Slow down when you approach a light. Even if it is green, do not speed up to pass through before it turns red. It may turn red before you reach, and you may be unable to brake in time. Drive in your lane. One who zigzags is a potential risk for himself and others. At a red light stand in the appropriate lane. Do not speed within city limits. Speed thrills. It also kills. Avoid driving close to buses and trucks. Allow sufficient place for buses to stop at bus stops.

Drive slowly near schools, hospitals and through crowded markets and other areas. Blow a horn only when necessary. Do not play loud music in the car. You may enjoy it, but you may not hear a horn or signal. Besides, it disturbs others. Do not drink and drive. Drinking affects one's perception of speed and space. It also slows down reactions in emergent conditions. Do not use cell phones while driving. This divides your attention. It can also affect your emotions. This can cause an accident.

If you drive a two-wheeler, use a helmet. In a car, use seat belts. If children are with you, ensure that they are secure in their seats. They can fall off when the brake is applied suddenly. Observe traffic rules. Be conscious of traffic signals. When in doubt, visit the nearest petrol pump and update yourself on traffic signs. Always be courteous on the road. Even if the other person is at fault, give him the benefit of doubt. There have been serious incidents of road rage.

It is not unusual to see some people take advantage of the open space, and extend their shops onto the road or even block it to hold a function. This is not without discomfort and inconvenience to the public. It is, therefore, against etiquette and the rules. If your need is urgent, and there is no alternative, inform the police and the civic authorities. Have a notice board announcing temporary closure. This way people will not object. A road is for everyone to use. Not for somebody to monopolise.

❏ ❏ ❏

27

Etiquette on the Highway

A highway is not like the roads within cities. Whereas roads within the city connect places together, a highway links several towns and cities.

Driving on the highway is not like driving on the roads within the city. Within city limits, the journey is short. On a highway, the journey is long. City roads are overcrowded. A highway is not. It is not possible to drive fast within the city. On the highway, traffic moves fast.

As we mentioned, speed thrills, but it also kills. One needs to be very careful about driving fast. Safety is paramount. Some highways are divided. Many are not. It is therefore necessary to drive on the proper side. Avoid overtaking, particularly on the bends. Many highways pass through villages and small towns. Slow down. Beware of children and village folk who may not be conscious of highway traffic. Do not brake suddenly. You could be hit by traffic from behind. If you need to stop, move off the highway. Keep away from fast-moving vehicles. Just as in other places, courtesy on the highway is important.

It is not unusual to come across closed railway crossings. Line up on your side of the road. This is the worst place to overtake. One wrong move and the others follow. When the gate opens, it will create chaos and confusion. It will then take longer to drive out of the mess. In the jam, you could damage your vehicle.

Many highways are not safe at night. Travel only if there is no alternative. Even then, be extra careful. Many trucks, tractor trolleys, and bullock-carts move in the dark without a light. They are a great risk to faster vehicles. Many accidental deaths are due to this single factor. Observe utmost care while driving on a highway. Etiquette is as important on the highway as elsewhere.

28

Parking Etiquette

Irresponsible parking is a matter of public concern. Each day, millions of people are put to discomfort and inconvenience for this single reason. We see it everywhere everyday. A person parks his car. When he returns later, a scooter is parked touching his rear bumper and a motorcycle is parked touching his front bumper. What should he do? We all know it is wrong. Yet we see it day after day in different combinations.

Parking lots are provided as a part of the civic infrastructure in every city. They may be located at the railway station, the bus terminal, outside hospitals, hotels, schools, colleges, near markets and other public places. A small charge may be collected for their use at some places. Sometimes parking may be free.

The important thing is that every vehicle owner needs parking space. Even public transport like auto-rickshaws, taxis and buses need parking areas.

In the interests of public convenience and safety, certain areas are designated as 'No Parking' zones. Do not ignore these rules. Penalties can be imposed for breaking rules.

To maintain parking etiquette, one needs to answer a simple question, "Will my vehicle obstruct someone's passage and cause inconvenience?" If the answer is, "Yes", you are parking in the wrong place.

Besides public convenience, vehicle safety is another aspect that must be considered. Many places clearly indicate,

'Parking at Owner's Risk'. This implies that the parking attendant is not responsible for a vehicle being damaged or stolen. In such cases, park properly and take precautions to ensure your vehicle is not damaged or stolen.

❑ ❑ ❑

29

Rail Travel Etiquette

Rail travel continues to be the most popular mode of travel in India. Millions of people use this facility every year. There are several classes of rail travel ranging from unreserved seats to reserved seats, first-class seats and berths, three-tier sleeper berths, three-tier air-conditioned, two-tier air-conditioned and first-class air-conditioned. Details of trains and available reservations and fares can now be accessed on the internet.

Reservations can be made through a nationwide computerised network. Special concessions are permissible to students, senior citizens and some other categories. At terminals, trains usually arrive on the platform at least 30 minutes before the scheduled departure. All coaches and seats are marked, with a passenger list displayed outside the door of reserved compartments. At the railway station, coolies are available to carry baggage. Their rates are fixed. However, they usually expect additional payment. Before boarding the coach, check the reservation list displayed on the door. A copy is also available at the station reservation board.

In air-conditioned classes of travel bed linen/blankets are provided. In first class and sleeper class, you need to carry your own bed linen. Keep your baggage secure with a chain and lock. Be particularly careful when the train stops at stations, especially during night halts. Attendants travel in some coaches. If you have any requirements, ask them. Tickets are checked en route, so keep them handy. Do not accept foodstuffs from strangers. In some classes, the ticket fare includes the meal charge. In other cases, you will need to buy food yourself. If the toilets are not clean, complain to the attendant. A complaint book is also available with him.

When you reach the destination, make sure you do not leave anything behind in the train.

❏ ❏ ❏

30

Air Travel Etiquette

Next to rail travel, air travel has become a popular mode of travelling for business or leisure travellers. It is the main mode of overseas travel. Those flying regularly usually deal with a travel agent. He can make reservations over the phone and even have the tickets delivered to your home. There are two classes of air travel, executive and economy.

You will need to arrive at least one or two hours before the flight, depending upon the airlines you are flying by, and whether it is a domestic or international flight. On arrival, you will need to check in. The airline will weigh and take your baggage. For economy class, 20 kg is permitted. You can carry one handbag only. A baggage receipt and a boarding pass bearing your seat number will be issued. Depending upon the time, you can then proceed for a security check, and wait in the lounge till the plane is ready.

At some airports, you can walk up directly to the plane. However, in most cases airline buses take you to the plane. If you have any problem climbing stairs, you need to advise the airline in advance.

Once inside the plane, you will be ushered to your seat. You can place the hand baggage in the overhead hold and sit with your seat erect and safety belt secured. Do not use any electronic equipment. It can interfere with the plane's signals. Once in place you will be offered candy. If you need earplugs, ask the airhostess for a pair. After take off, you can recline your seat. During flight you will be served refreshments, lunch or dinner, depending upon the duration of the flight. International flights offer music, movies and in-flight shopping, too.

During touch down, be seated with the seat belt in position until the plane taxis to a halt. There may only be one or two exits. Be patient. Thank the staff as you leave. A bus will take you to the terminal. Collect your baggage at the baggage hold.

❑ ❑ ❑

31

Etiquette During Holidays

It has become a part of life to go on regular holidays for rest and recreation. It is a getaway from the monotony of routine life. It gives an opportunity to visit new places and make new friends. It is also an occasion to do things one cannot indulge in because of time constraints.

It may just be a picnic, a weekend away from home, or a prolonged visit to a holiday resort. Enjoy what you do. Relax. Get rid of the tension of daily life.

The simplest form of a holiday is a picnic to a nearby park, lake, river or scenic spot. Even if such locales are not within driving distance, one can still go out of town to a nearby village and spend a few hours in the rural environment under a shady tree! But wherever you go, good etiquette and manners will count. Leave the place as clean and undisturbed as it was before you went there. Even if there were paper and plastic bags when you went there, collect and throw these into a dustbin, if one is available. If not, collect these in a bag to throw away later when you come across a dustbin on the way home.

In case you are a smoker, ensure you do not carelessly throw a lit matchstick or a lighted cigarette stub. Many devastating fires have been caused accidentally through sheer carelessness.

A holiday over the weekend is something in between a picnic and a longer holiday. While it aims at providing some time away from the normal routine, it is invariably planned at short notice. The venue should be within easy reach, say a travelling time of two to four hours at the most.

On such a trip you will need to carry clothes for the overnight stay. Keep luggage to the minimum. Make arrangements for an overnight stay. Either visit a place where accommodation is easy to find or have a place booked in advance over the phone. Most hotels do provide bedding. If you are going to a place where there are no hotels, you will need to carry bedding.

The annual holiday requires more elaborate planning. When the whole family is involved in the planning, it can be great fun. On an annual holiday, there will be many considerations. The budget, the place you wish to visit, hotel reservations, and other travel and stay arrangements need to be taken care of before you leave home.

Avoid disappointment and inconvenience by making advance reservations. Advance rail bookings, hotel reservations and sightseeing arrangements keep you tension free. When making reservations be precise about the time and date of your arrival and departure, the kind of accommodation required, the number of people accompanying you and other relevant details. Make part payment in advance and get confirmations in writing by letter or fax. Travel arrangements must also be confirmed.

On arrival at the hotel you will be required to enter your details on the guest register or on a separate guest information form. Verify details of tariffs and taxes, and the adjustment of advance payment. If you wish to pay through credit card, inquire beforehand whether the hotel accepts your credit card. The bellboy carrying the baggage will usher you to your room. He will expect a tip.

Most hotels have telephones in every room. A card placed next to the telephone gives details of numbers to be dialled to reach services like room service, housekeeping, reception, laundry etc. The restaurants in the hotel may have specific times within which they serve meals. Not all hotels have 24-hour service. If you need special service, check at the reception.

Advance reservations make holidays pleasurable.

Before using STD facilities on the telephone, check hotel charges. Some hotels hike the rates to exorbitant levels. It might be cheaper to use a public call office outside the hotel.

It you are expecting visitors, instruct the reception whether you want them sent to your room, or would like them to wait in the lounge. Some posh restaurants have a dress code for diners. You may need to wear a proper suit and tie, if male, and saris or an evening gown, if female. Casual dresses like T-shirts and jeans are not permitted. Inquire about these and take care to follow the dress code to avoid any argument or embarrassment. If you are inviting guests to the restaurant, do advise them accordingly.

Every hotel expects guests to observe good etiquette and manners. Do not throw litter in the common areas like the lounge, restaurants or passages. After reading magazines and newspapers kept in the lounge, return these to their original place. Do not talk too loudly, or permit the children to run about, disturbing other guests. At all times during your stay, you need to be considerate towards the other guests.

Many guests are guilty of stealing hotel property on the pretext of collecting mementoes. Hotels are aware of this tendency and have a security system to counteract it. Please avoid pilfering hotel items. If caught, it could be very embarrassing.

When you wish to check out, inform the reception some time in advance. They will have the bills ready so that you do not have to wait. The bellboy will have your baggage in the reception, and place it in the vehicle taking you to the airport or railway station. Remember to tip the bellboy.

. ❏ ❏ ❏

32

The Etiquette
of Introductions

Many people are guilty of failing to introduce one person to another. And more often, there are people who fail to make introductions altogether. If two persons known to you, but unknown to each other, meet for a fleeting moment on the road, it may be all right if you do not introduce them. However, if it is at a party, or on another occasion when the meeting is for some length of time, it is appropriate to introduce one to the other.

Even when you are in doubt whether they know each other, or have been introduced earlier, it will do no harm if you introduce them saying, "I wonder if you have met...." It would be in good taste, and will help even a shy person be at ease with others almost immediately.

As with all things, there are certain rules about making introductions. Introduce a younger person to an elder person, a gent to a lady, a subordinate to a senior, an immediate relative to an outsider. Different occasions will require some variations. They can be adjusted by combining the simple rules.

While making introductions, do not hurry it over. Take your time. Announce the names clearly so that the other person can register this easily. Sometimes it may be useful to add special qualifications or qualities of the person like, "Please meet Sonali. She is a wonderful cook," or "This is Satish. He is a commercial artist with...." Such remarks about a person make for easy conversation amongst new friends. Everyone will appreciate your helping them make friends.

All introductions are not expected to develop into lasting friendships. On being introduced, a simple "How do you do?" or "Pleased to meet you," or its Indian version said with folded hands meets the requirements of the moment. If you are interested, you could converse on subjects of mutual interest. It could develop into a lasting friendship.

33

Etiquette with Neighbours

Neighbours can be your best friends – and sometimes enemies too! It all depends upon the kind of relationship you wish to build with them.

When you look at individuals, you find that they are all good people. Only when you start interacting with them, and personal self-interest intervenes, problems begin to surface. It is the same with neighbours. As long as everyone minds his own business, and does not step on each other's toes, it is fine. All good relationships are built upon this truth.

Share happiness with the neighbours. Do not share problems. If you have problems of common interest, sit together and discuss how they can be resolved. If something went wrong because of your fault, apologise. Saying "sorry" should come as easily as saying "thank you".

As neighbours, work out plans to promote harmony and happiness in the area. Cooperate with each other. Do not compete for petty things. When the neighbour is away, it is your responsibility to receive guests, or messages and mail. It is for you to protect their interests in their absence. When you do a good deed, they will reciprocate. Like them, you too may need to go outstation.

Neighbourhood gossip does the worst damage to good neighbourly relations. Just when you are working hard to establish a happy relationship, gossip can undo all the good.

Avoid gossip. Avoid criticism. Look at relationships with a positive attitude. A neighbour should be a friend who lives next door. Help and look after each other's interest both in good times and when trouble strikes. Live and let live should be the guiding spirit. Good etiquette and manners strengthen relationships between neighbours.

❑ ❑ ❑

34

Etiquette with Senior Citizens

With better healthcare the number of senior citizens is on the increase. Many of them planned well in advance, and then settled comfortably to spend their twilight years. Some are not very fortunate. They may have lost their spouse or need some support. Whatever it may be, everyone appreciates that senior citizens are worthy of special attention.

One should never forget the simple fact that each one of us has to reach old age one day and face the same problems – physically, mentally, emotionally or financially – that today's senior citizens face. Those who showered love and affection on their children usually have little to worry about. They are enjoying the fruits of the trees they planted in their younger years. They are well cared for and happy. But many are not so blessed. They may be financially all right, but need emotional support. This can best come from the family. If they give it today, it will come back to them when they are old. Many are not enjoying good health and need special care. The family can best provide this.

A serious setback that many senior citizens feel is lack of self-esteem. They feel they are no longer wanted. Perhaps they do not have enough to contribute to society. This is not true. Every senior citizen can boast of a lifetime of experience. In this long span of life they have acquired special skills and knowledge. If everyone can make them realise this fact, many of their problems would be solved. Many social service organisations are doing this.

In our country, age is respected. If everyone can extend a little more care to senior citizens through good etiquette and manners in everyday life, life would be easier and happier for everyone.

35

Etiquette with Important People

$\mathbf{W}$e are not new to the art of according regard and respect to those who are elder to us or senior. Elders are specially respected with exclusive greetings and the touching of feet.

Our respect is evident when the suffix *ji* is added to the relationship or name. Instead of using the English equivalent of father and mother as daddy and mummy, it is common to hear *daddyji* and *mummyji*. Similarly, instead of addressing a person by his surname as Mr Sharma, it is common for him to be addressed as *Sharmaji*.

The British gave India another suffix, *sahib*. It literally means 'sir'. It is derived from the Arabic word that denotes *friend*. Again, instead of addressing him plainly as Mr Sharma, as a mark of respect we say *Sharma sahib* or *Sharmasaab*.

Besides personal respect, in the interests of good etiquette and manners, our speech should be laced with these suffixes or prefixes. Whenever in doubt, it is common to use 'sir' for gents and 'madam' or 'ma'am' for ladies.

However, there may be instances when one is at a loss about how to address persons in important positions. The President of India and the Governors of the states are addressed by the words *Your Excellency* or *His Excellency*. These words are in vogue since British times. In Hindi, the equivalent for the word President is *Rashtrapatiji*. The equivalent for governor is *Rajyapalji*.

Senior judges are addressed by using the prefix *Honourable Justice*. For example, the Chief Justice of the Supreme Court of India would be addressed as *Honourable Chief Justice of India*, followed by his name. The judges would be addressed as *Honourable Justice* (name) *of the Supreme Court of India*. The chief justice and the judges of the High Courts of various states would also be addressed in the same manner. At the district level, the head of the judiciary is the District and Sessions Judge.

The Prime Minister is addressed as *Honourable Prime Minister* and ministers as *Honourable Minister of...* Similarly, at the state level, the Chief Minister is addressed as the *Honourable Chief Minister* and ministers as *Honourable Minister for...*

When you need to deal with diplomats, the ambassadors and High Commissioners are addressed as *His Excellency, the Ambassador of...*

In our country we have almost all religions of the world. In each religion, those in senior positions are addressed in different ways. Whenever you need to interact with them, inquire how they are to be addressed. In case of doubt, use the word *Sir*. In Hindu temples, those conducting ceremonies are referred to as *pujaris* or *pandits*. Those who have renounced worldly life, marked by the wearing of white, yellow or saffron clothes are addressed as *swamiji*. The head of a sect is addressed as *mahantji*. In a higher position we have a *mandaleshwar*. In a still higher position, we have *mahamandaleshwar*. Whenever in doubt about one's designation, address them as *Swamiji* or *Maharajji*.

Just as we have the prefixes Mr and Mrs when addressing individuals, amongst Hindus one uses *Shri* and *Shrimati*. When addressing Hindu religious heads, it is common to use the prefix *Shri Shri 108...* or *Shri Shri 1008* (*Shri* is always repeated in this instance), depending upon the position of the person.

In everyday life when you need to interact with a person in a senior position, it would be appropriate to address the person by the position he holds. For example, the mayor would be addressed as *Honourable Mayor*. Whenever in doubt, always address a senior person as 'Sir' and a senior lady as 'Madam'. This exemplifies good manners.

❏ ❏ ❏

36

Etiquette with Foreign Visitors

With people travelling all over the world, it has become common to meet and receive foreign visitors as guests. Guests are guests and will need special attention. However, living standards, customs and food habits vary from one place to another. To make foreign guests comfortable, one will need to understand these differences.

They are very sensitive about time. If you tell them that you will pick them from their hotel at 10.00 AM, it means 10.00 AM. It does not mean around 10.00 AM. They can take offence at your negligence of time. If for some unavoidable reason you are delayed, please convey it by telephone.

When you invite them to your home, please explain what the occasion is all about. They would like to dress to suit the occasion. Otherwise they may be casually dressed and feel embarrassed if it is a special occasion and everyone is formally dressed.

When you offer them food or drinks, accept their response. If they say 'No', it means that they would not like anything. If they say 'Yes', tell them the choice that is available. You do not need to go out of the way to prepare the food they eat in their country. Foreigners relish Indian food. Offer whatever is available. Do not insist on piling food on their plates. Do not also force them to eat dishes they do not want to try. They are sensitive to heavy, spicy food. Unless they ask for spicy dishes, do not ply them with this. They are also sensitive to 'normal' drinking water. Offer mineral water or soft drinks, instead.

In case you are offering them home hospitality, make sure you provide them suitable accommodation where they can enjoy comfort and privacy. The bed linen must be clean and fresh. They are used to western-style toilets. Keep a roll of toilet paper in the loo. If such arrangements are not possible, make reservations for their stay in a hotel with the necessary facilities. You can inquire about the hotel tariff that would suit their budget.

If you take them out for sightseeing, do not overload the vehicle. If a car is for four passengers, accommodate only four persons in it. Do not make it too hectic for your guests. If they seem tired and have no interest in what you are showing them, take them back home or wherever they are putting up. In changed environments, particularly in warm weather, fatigue builds up faster.

If you take them out shopping, visit establishments that do fair business. Foreign visitors can be very suspicious. If they feel cheated, they may blame you for taking them there. Even if they visit a shop of their own choice, and you feel that the salesperson is overcharging, bring it to their notice immediately. Ask the shopkeeper why he is quoting a higher price. If you feel he is unfair, suggest an alternate shop.

It is normal practice in many countries to hold hands, embrace or even kiss on the cheek as a show of personal affection. Do not interpret it in any other way, although you may find it embarrassing.

Sometimes the guests may inquire whether you require anything from their country. Do not jump at the offer and ask for favours or gifts. You may feel it is justified as a measure of reciprocity. It is not. If they wish to offer a gift in response to your hospitality, it is their choice. Good etiquette does not permit you to seek it.

Your guests will carry the memories you help generate during their stay with you. If they have enjoyed your hospitality and liked it, they will get back to you through a letter or e-mail when they return home. Respond immediately by telling them how much you enjoyed their visit and that you look forward to their next visit.

❑ ❑ ❑

37

Etiquette of Exchanging Gifts

A gift is a token of thoughtfulness for a person. It gives happiness to both, the one who gives it, and the one who receives it. For the sheer happiness that it gives everyone, we find people giving and receiving gifts throughout the year – on birthdays and anniversaries, during festivals and special days like Diwali, Raksha Bandhan, Bhaiya Duj, Valentine's Day, Mother's Day, and Father's Day. Even on other occasions, gifts are exchanged.

At Diwali and New Year, many corporate gifts are passed on to employees, customers, clients and others. The etiquette of giving and receiving gifts requires that one should not assess or ascertain the value of a gift in monetary terms. The purpose of the gift is defeated when one feels it should have been something else. A gift is a token of thoughtfulness. It need not be something costly or a thing that we needed. A gift is meant to remind one of the emotional bonds of the person who has presented it.

When one carries a bouquet of flowers for a sick person, it is not presented because the sick person needs it, but simply to cheer him up. Flowers reflect the glory of God. Their fragrance lifts up the spirits. Can any of these qualities be evaluated with money?

Never "recycle" gifts. People sometimes exchange gifts only for the sake of doing so. Often, during festivals like Diwali and New Year, gifts received the previous year are taken out of the closet, dusted, gift-wrapped and presented to friends and relatives. Occasionally, this can cause a lot of embarrassment. I once received a Diwali gift from a relative, which I had presented to them the previous year! Avoid recycling gifts and falling into this trap.

Give voluntarily and with pleasure. Receive with gracious happiness. Think about the sentiments of the person who thought of you and brought a gift for you. Gift-wrapping adds value to any gift. Do not skip this – even if it is something for your wife or child. When you receive a gift, say "Thank you" with a smile.

❏ ❏ ❏

38

Etiquette in the Park

Parks are often referred to as lungs of the city. While planning new colonies, it is mandatory to provide parks for people to relax and walk around, and for children to play. They provide open space for a lot of activities.

Parks are public property. Unfortunately, our concept of public property is that everyone has a right to use it, but it is someone else's responsibility to maintain it! We must realise that it is every user's responsibility to look after and maintain the park, since it is a happy meeting ground for everyone in the locality.

It is everyone's responsibility to keep a park clean. Hawkers and vendors should not be permitted inside the park. Civic bodies that own the parkland do have some maintenance activity. If this is lacking, consider it your responsibility to bring it to the notice of the authorities. Inform the local councillor from your area.

If there are flowers, shrubs and trees in the park, ensure these are well maintained. So that the grass is not damaged, use walkways for walking and jogging, if these have been provided. If a urinal has been provided in some corner of the park, ensure it is used properly and kept clean. Those who bring their pets to the park should make sure that other users are not inconvenienced.

If the park is used for some public activity like a *puja* or *jagrata* or some similar activity, it is the responsibility of the organisers to leave the place clean after use.

❏ ❏ ❏

39

Etiquette at the Movie Theatre

The need for good etiquette begins the moment you enter the premises of a cinema theatre. Since you will be away for three hours, have your vehicle parked safely and ensure it does not cause anyone any inconvenience.

Do not hesitate to stand in a queue for the tickets. It will not hurt your self-esteem. When the theatre doors open to allow the audience in, do not rush or push others. In all city theatres the seats are marked. Occupy your own seats. In case of any difficulty, seek the help of the usher. Once seated, do not keep talking to your companions about the movie or other things in general. Do not cheer, shout or pass comments. All this can disturb others. Do not push the seat in front of you, or nudge the person next to you. If a woman is sitting next to you, ensure your elbow or hand does not intrude onto her portion of the seat, accidentally or otherwise.

If children are accompanying you, ensure that they do not shout, talk or cry. Some parents permit their children to run up and down the aisle. This can be very disturbing to others.

During the show, your cellular phone should be switched off or put on vibrating mode. If it is necessary to attend to the call, go out of the hall and speak in the lobby. This will not disturb or inconvenience other viewers.

Smoking is not permitted in movie theatres. If you must smoke, go outside. Smoke only where it is permitted. When in doubt, ask the usher.

Carrying eatables and drinks into the hall is prohibited in some theatres. Observe these rules. When permitted, eat quietly. Avoid talking loudly or making a noise passing eatables to your companions. Do not litter the theatre with wrappers or peanut shells. Do not leave water bottles in the passageway. Do remember that there is another show after you leave. The new audience would like to enter a clean hall. Throw wrappers into dustbins.

Do not spit *paan* (beetle juice) on the seats and walls inside the premises. It is improper and unhygienic. When using the toilet, observe rules of using public toilets.

When the show ends, do not rush out. Within the next few minutes everyone will be out. In the rush one can push or hurt somebody. Fellow viewers will appreciate your following proper etiquette even at a movie theatre.

❑ ❑ ❑

40

Etiquette in
a Restaurant

Many people like to eat in a restaurant occasionally. Most restaurants offer a variety of items to suit everyone. However, in larger cities there are specialty restaurants offering regional specialties, or exotic cuisine like Chinese, Thai and continental.

On arrival at an upmarket restaurant, the steward greets one. He may inquire about the number of people in the group so that an appropriate table can be suggested. During rush hours when the restaurant is overcrowded, the steward may request you to wait until a table falls vacant. Maintain your cool on such occasions.

Once seated, the steward will place menu cards before the group so that the order can be placed. Most restaurants offer *a la carte* services. This means that you can choose the dishes from the menu card and pay for each dish. Sometimes a buffet spread is also offered at a fixed price per person. You can eat as much as you like from the dishes spread out on the table.

The steward may first inquire if you would like to order something to drink. If you do, order accordingly. In any case, the waiter will place water before every person. If you like soup, order that first. With soup, you may like to order some snacks. If you do not want soup, you could proceed to order the whole meal. Some prefer to order individual items; others prefer to order jointly. Most of the dishes in a restaurant are big. One person cannot eat all of it unless the dish is planned for an individual only. If in doubt about anything, ask the steward. On most occasions, a joint order is placed and dishes shared. This avoids wastage.

While the order is being prepared, the waiter will lay the table. He will also place salad, pickle, chutney and ketchup to be savoured with the meal. When the dishes are brought in, the waiter may offer to serve everyone. He could also leave these on the table so that everyone can help himself or herself. After assessing the quantity, if additional food is required, the additional order can be placed.

During the meal if you wish to call the waiter, catch the eye of the nearest waiter or steward, and pass your request. It is discourteous to shout out for him. It will only attract the attention of everyone in the restaurant towards you.

The napkin is generally placed in the lap. Depending on the kind of food, it can be eaten with a fork and knife, or a fork and spoon. Items like *chapatti, naan,* bread, etc that need to be eaten with the hand should be eaten that way. After the meal, the waiter will bring warm water in a bowl to rinse hands. Wipe them dry with the napkin. In the West, a crushed napkin is indicative of a very enjoyable meal.

During the meal, it is customary to place the cutlery with the tips of the fork and knife pointing at each other like the sides of the alphabet 'A'. On completing the meal, the cutlery is placed straight in the middle of the plate like the alphabet 'H'. The waiter will then clear the plate.

The dessert is ordered after the meal. If you prefer coffee to dessert, or want both, you could order accordingly. Once the meal is over, you could ask the waiter for the bill. You can pay cash or by credit card, if acceptable. Whichever way you pay, leave an appropriate tip for the waiter. Besides the tip, you could compliment the waiter for good service, if this were the case.

If for any reason whatsoever you are not pleased with the food or service, or with a particular dish, do not lose your cool. Ask the waiter to call the steward and pass your complaint to him in a businesslike manner. This way your complaint will be looked into immediately. If not satisfied, avoid visiting the place again.

On your way out if the steward is at the door, say a polite, "Thank you" with a smile. Courtesy motivates everyone to serve well.

❑ ❑ ❑

41

Etiquette at a Club

A club is a place where people get together to meet each other and enjoy common interests like indoor or outdoor games. Most clubs also have bar and restaurant facilities. When you enter the club premises, the host will enter your names in the guest register. As a guest your responsibility is that of being a gracious guest.

As a club member, one is bound by the rules of the club. These rules are periodically amended to suit the needs of the members. A managing committee elected annually by the club members administers the club.

Most clubs have a card room, billiard room, table tennis, swimming pool, squash, badminton and tennis courts. Clubs also have a library and reading room. Besides these, there will be a bar and a restaurant. Some clubs have residential rooms for guests. There are separate rules for the use of all these facilities. Members will need to follow these rules.

In a club one interacts with a variety of persons coming from diverse backgrounds, businesses and professions. To ensure good etiquette and manners, follow the simple rules of getting along with people. To be immediately likeable, be humble. Everyone appreciates humility. Do not show off or act pompous. Do not act tough with members or the club staff. A club is a joint property. Follow club rules.

If you are aggrieved about any club service, talk to the appropriate person. If your complaint is not redressed, take up the matter with the managing committee.

❏ ❏ ❏

42

Shopping Etiquette

"Civility costs nothing and buys everything."

– Lady M.W. Montague

If you want to be a smart shopper, you must learn to be a welcome customer. A shopkeeper is obliged to serve all customers. However, there are some who always receive the best attention. It is not that the shopkeeper is going to make additional profit from that person. It is just a matter of good human relations. A good-natured person is welcome everywhere.

Do not make shopping a serious round of the market. A smile here, a greeting there, and the usual courtesy of saying, "thank you" take one a long way. A gentle disposition always ensures happy shopping.

When you go shopping, be precise about what you wish to purchase. Prices are marked on all items. If not satisfied, try other shops. Compare prices. Buy what you feel is value for money. Do not criticise a shopkeeper or his goods. If you have a genuine complaint, bring it to his notice in a businesslike manner. Recognise his constraints. He will do his best to satisfy you.

As far as practical, buy regular home requirements from a set of shopkeepers who offer good value for money. This way you build good relationships. You get the best offers and find that your shopping experience is always a happy one.

❏ ❏ ❏

43

Etiquette in Places of Worship

India has numerous places of worship – temples, mosques, gurudwaras, churches, fire temples and synagogues, amongst others. Many natural resources are held sacred too. A large number of homes may also have temples or a place devoted to prayer. There is an equally big variety of religious customs and rituals. They may range from religious ceremonies at the birth of a child to *mundan* or sacred thread ceremony, or ceremonies at weddings, special remembrances and deaths. Each occasion requires certain etiquette to be maintained.

In most cases, footwear is considered unclean and is not permitted in places of prayer. In many places, like gurudwaras and mosques, it is mandatory that the head be covered. Some use a turban, others a cap or scarf. One sits on the ground. Therefore, depending upon personal convenience, one should be appropriately dressed.

Many times, your personal presence and attention may be all that is required. However, on some occasions, you may need to carry flowers, incense sticks, a coconut, sweets, and similar items for prayer. When in doubt, observe others. Look out for local customs and rituals. Follow others.

When the ceremony is in progress, observe self-restraint and silence. Do not disturb the ceremony, or those sitting near you. If *prasad* is served in the end, accept it in your right hand supported by the left hand. If *tilak* is applied, and you are not wearing a turban or cap, cover your head with the left hand.

When departing from a prayer meeting held in memory of a deceased person, it is customary to meet the bereaved family with folded hands. Nothing need be said. Your expression should convey your sentiments.

44

Etiquette at a Death Ceremony

Death is an inevitable part of life. It marks the end of one's journey of life on Earth. The death of a near one makes us realise this fact more strongly.

When receiving a call about a person's demise, do convey your grief to the caller. Inquire about the time and place of cremation. You should wear white or light-coloured clothes. They should look sober on you. Avoid taking children with you, as they may not realise the solemnity of the occasion and create noise and distractions. Besides, watching elders crying and wailing, the children may be disturbed emotionally.

Your behaviour on such an occasion should be serene. Do not speak loudly or more than is necessary. Switch your cellular phone to silent mode. Ensure you do not interrupt the activities or ceremonies in any way. Offer to help the bereaved family in some way. At this time particularly, they need mental and emotional support.

If you are unable to go during the time of cremation due to unavoidable circumstances, visit the family as soon as possible. When you do go over, while conveying your condolences, do tell them the reason for your inability to go earlier.

45

Etiquette at Public Toilets

"Good manners are made up of petty sacrifices."

– Emerson

Everybody needs to use public toilets. We find them everywhere. In the trains, at bus terminals, at airports, in parks, shopping plazas, restaurants and hotels. They are provided as a public convenience. Life would be difficult without them.

Do we use these utilities in the way we should? Do we leave them clean and dry, as we would like to find them when we use them? Like all public property, everyone wants to use them, but does not want to be responsible for their maintenance.

Since the frequency of use of these toilets is very high compared to toilets in a home, the authorities maintaining these do provide special care. However, a little care and consideration by users can make the work easier for everyone.

Simple rules apply to the use of public toilets. Use the urinal and toilet seats properly. Flush after use. In an English toilet, men should always remember to raise the toilet seat before urinating. If you have used an English toilet to evacuate your bowels, there will be a roll of toilet paper provided to clean up. You could use this, instead of water. If you are more comfortable using toilet paper, carry some with you. It is not available in all public toilets.

If there is shortage of water, lodge a complaint about it. After washing hands, leave the soap in a soap dish or in a dry place. Do not leave the tap flowing. Do not spill water around the toilet seat. When people enter with dirty shoes, it leaves the toilet muddy. A little consideration on your part can make these public places cleaner and more comfortable for everyone.

❑ ❑ ❑

46

Etiquette in the Office

An office is a place from where a business or professional organisation operates. It may have a few workers operating from a single room, or it may be a vast organisation with several departments, and employing a large number of persons in different capacities. The office has a definite purpose. It is there to provide a service that is directly linked with the purpose of the organisation.

Every office operates with a certain discipline. Some rules are written. Many are not. Those which are not, come within the working style or custom developed over a working period. This is referred to as office etiquette.

Every office has its own standards of time consciousness. The organisation expects its employees to be in their workplaces at a particular time, diligently put in a certain number of working hours, and leave at the appointed time. It is important to fulfil these time standards.

Every office also has a customary standard of dress for its employees. In some offices, it is mandatory that the men wear neckties. Lady employees may be required to wear saris, salwar-kameez or slacks. In many offices, there may be no recommended standards of dress. However, it is still expected that men will not turn up in the office wearing jeans and T-shirts. Similarly, low-neck blouses and mini-skirts worn by lady employees will not be appreciated.

Every office also has its own recommendation pertaining to smoking by the employees. Some permit it. Many do not. Even where smoking is permitted, there may be rules about smoking at one's desk, or in the rest room. If smoking is permitted, follow the simple etiquette of smoking. Have an ashtray on your table.

Every office also has a working culture pertaining to handling of documents, files, office equipment and stationery. Every employee must understand it. It is in the employee's interest to ensure that every evening the table is clear, documents have been filed, the files have been placed inside cabinets and the stationery is back in the employee's table drawer.

Some offices serve midday tea or coffee. Many do not. In some offices the employees pool in to have coffee and tea served. In others, they order the office attendant to get it from a canteen, or stall. This is midday refreshment, and not an occasion to leave one's table to have a little chat. Employees bring in their own lunch in most offices. However, hot cases are provided sometimes. In some offices, the executives are served lunch.

A small office is provided with a single toilet. Both men and women use it. Larger offices provide separate toilets for men and women. Many people use these toilets daily. Every person using the toilet must leave it clean and dry.

People at all levels work in an office. At the top, there will be the chairman or managing director. Then the general manager and other senior managers in-charge of separate departments, middle level managers and junior managers follow. Personal assistants and office staff will assist them. At each level, one will be responsible to a senior person. Simultaneously, one will be responsible for persons in subordinate positions. Irrespective of what position one holds, every employee must remember that they are part of a team. When everyone fulfils his responsibility, the team succeeds. If one person is careless, the whole team may suffer.

At every level, except the very top, you will report to a senior. Most seniors understand human nature well.

However, sometimes one does come across a boss who is difficult to please. A boss will be a boss. Observe self-restraint. Be patient. If he gets angry easily or hurls unfair criticism, do not talk back. Do not grumble behind his back. He may be more proficient in his line of specialisation than at understanding human problems. Try to understand what he desires and why. If your performance is lacking, analyse your shortcomings. Accept mistakes. Tact and patience can be very useful tools.

The boss is always a boss. Respect him.

Keep the senior management happy. Your future progress depends upon them. Some use flattery and other devious means. Such progress does not last. The senior management have their eyes set only on productivity and profitability. There is much that one can learn from seniors. If you have your eye on a senior position, two things are important – the ability to learn new skills and the willingness to shoulder responsibility.

When the management approves of your efforts, do not take all the credit. Share it with the staff. Your modesty will bring in still better results. When something goes wrong, step forward and take responsibility. Ensure it is not repeated.

While dealing with colleagues, be cordial, friendly and helpful. Ensure there is harmony amongst all. Even if each fulfils a different responsibility, work as a team. If someone lags behind, offer support. Never impose yourself on others. If you do, they will try to pull you down in your weaker moments. If you are capable, the management will shortlist you for a promotion.

Treat subordinates with respect and guide them in their responsibilities. If they sometimes make mistakes, do not criticise them before others. Talk to them in private. Explain why you are feeling let down. Also suggest how he could make amends.

Don't criticise a subordinate openly. Talk to him privately.

As a senior, be fair to all subordinates. While handling complaints or breakdown of discipline, be understanding, but firm. Spell out your stand in clear terms. There will always be occasions when people break discipline, irrespective of their positions. Handle such situations tactfully but firmly.

An office is a place to work, not romance.

The telephone is a popular service that is misused. Phones are installed to promote the business. If employees have direct access to them, this does not mean they can misuse them. It is good etiquette not to use the phone for outgoing calls without permission of the person in-charge. Ensure your incoming personal calls are only for urgent messages. Do not forget that whenever a telephone is in personal use, it is not available for office use. If each employee were to use it for a few minutes per day, the total time would run into hours.

Computers are a common sight in offices nowadays. Internet connections are also provided at many places. There is a tendency to misuse these facilities for personal gain, such as by playing computer games, chatting online with friends, visiting websites not related to office work, shopping online and accessing personal e-mails. Such activities lead to a decline in efficiency, loss of office hours, increase in telephone bills and, finally, a decrease in the profits of the company. Moreover, if you are caught in such acts by the management, it can cause a lot of embarrassment. So, ensure you do not breach office discipline and etiquette by misusing your computer.

Employees also misuse office time. On some pretext, they may go out to do personal work. They may invite people to the office and spend time in small talk. Or they may spend time in gossip. Avoid misusing office time in such ways. You are being paid for the time you put in. When you misuse office hours, you are stealing time. If your personal work is urgent, there are provisions for leave. Or you could seek permission from your boss to come in a little late or leave early on that particular day. You could offer to make up for the lost time by coming in earlier or staying late the next day.

Do not flirt or socialise in the office.

Office discipline is also affected when employees begin to misuse office equipment like calculators, typewriters, fax machines, computers, printers, photocopiers and other equipment. Office furniture is another item of abuse. The replacement costs for all these can be very high. It is good etiquette to look after the equipment entrusted to you by the management, which they will always appreciate.

Not everyone is entitled to use office vehicles. If you are, please use it for official purposes only. Similarly, entertainment allowances are strictly for professional use.

When men and women work together, there can be gender-related problems. While everyone has a personal life, this should not be mixed with professional activities. Having affairs in the office is bad for your image and future prospects in the company.

Another gender-related problem is sexual harassment, which exists in much greater proportion than many are willing to admit. Some companies have definite guidelines to preclude this. If male, ensure you do not try to take undue advantage of female colleagues. If female, ensure you do not use feminine wiles to push your career graph.

There must be a definite policy for working late in the evening. If lady employees need to stay late, arrangements must be made to drop them back home safely.

The most important aspect of office etiquette is how clients and others are attended to. Business is people. They are the purpose of the office. If customers are not attended to speedily, it creates a bad impression.

A receptionist must always be prompt and courteous.

The first person a client meets in the office is the receptionist. Often, she has the dual role of receiving visitors and also attending the telephone. If so, she should always be polite, prompt and courteous with everyone. All telephone inquiries must be answered or redirected promptly.

Do not keep visitors waiting without reason.

We spend almost one-third of our working lives in the workplace. The etiquette we follow at work reflects in our everyday life. We are accepted in life in keeping with the image we project at work. Good etiquette and manners in office go a long way in projecting the right image for employees as well as the company.

❏ ❏ ❏

47

Job-hunting Etiquette

If you are looking for a job, good etiquette and manners will make your journey shorter. All employers seek workers who are disciplined. Good manners can be perceived immediately. Good work follows later.

The purpose of all jobs is the same – to fulfil a human need. In most cases, the fulfilment of a particular need may not result in a financial gain to the employer directly. It may just be one link in a long process where many people are working at a variety of occupations to eventually offer a good product or service. Unless you fulfil the responsibilities to benefit him with your work, his purpose of employing you will be in vain.

When you come across a job advertisement, first understand its requirements. Most advertisements are brief due to space constraints, but still provide sufficient information for prospective candidates to assess the requirements.

If you feel you can meet the job requirements efficiently, do apply. For this, you will have to draft your first communication with the prospective employer. Many employers require the initial application to be made on a prescribed form that they supply on request or on payment. In most cases, though, it is absolutely in order to apply on a plain white sheet of paper, neatly typewritten, or hand-written. If you have a personal letterhead that is not too fancy or ostentatious, use it. But do not use business letterheads or fancy paper.

Do remember one thing – the prospective employer wants to hire somebody who can help him further his business interests. So you could only secure the job if you can convince him that he will benefit by employing you.

Initially, the application forms will be screened to decide which candidates to call for the interview. Therefore, your application must also convey that you are worthy of being called for an interview, by making a fair representation of your qualifications and capabilities, with particular emphasis on the job requirements. Mention details about your academic career, extra-curricular activities and achievements, jobs held, or experience, if any. Be modest about your achievements. Do not give any incorrect or false information. Copies of certificates must support the information about your qualifications and achievements. Originals can be shown during the interview.

Keep the application brief and to the point. If you cannot have the application composed, have it neatly handwritten. Make certain the handwriting is absolutely neat, clear and legible in order to create a good impression. If the application is on a prescribed form, fill it neatly. Avoid overwriting or crowding. Keep a copy of the application for your personal record.

If the prospective employer has mentioned it, mark the envelope with specific remarks like "For Management Trainees", "Junior Executives", etc, so that it reaches the right department immediately.

If the application fulfils all basic requirements, the chances are you will receive an interview call. Get to know all that you can about the employer, his company and the job. If possible, also find out all about the responsibilities of the post applied for. Such information can be garnered from advertisements in the media, house journals, local distributors, and even local retailers. You will then be better able to gauge the prospective employer's needs and be better positioned to answer questions at the interview.

Do acknowledge the interview call and confirm the place, day and time mentioned in the letter.

The prospective employer will use the interview to assess the image each candidate projects of himself. The employer will keenly observe your poise, manners and sense of dress. He will also reconfirm the facts you mentioned in your application and gauge your general knowledge, special interests and achievements, the ability to learn new skills, and your attitude towards the kind of job he can offer. He may also want to know about your past successes and failures, and how you faced them. Your reactions and answers to these questions will help him draw conclusions about your suitability for the post.

You must reach the interview venue at the appointed time. Dress appropriately. One's sense of dress reveals a lot about one's personality. The dress should not be too formal or too casual. Wear a day suit, or if the weather and circumstances do not permit it, a white shirt and coloured pant with a necktie will be all right. Wear either brown or black shoes to match the pant. Avoid fancy footwear. Ensure you shave, have clean nails and properly groomed hair. Carry documents neatly in a file.

Remain calm before the interview.

At the venue, do not chat up the receptionist or compare notes with other candidates. Do not smoke either. You can read the newspaper or a book, while you await your interview. When called in, remember that first impressions are crucial. So enter with a smile. Sit down when asked to. Let the interviewer open the conversation. He may ask you to tell him something about yourself. Be brief and to the point.

Gradually, he will come to the more pertinent questions. Answer in simple language to convey a clear meaning. Remember that your power of expression is being tested. The interviewer may want to test your reactions in special circumstances and ask provocative questions or broach controversial topics. Exercise great tact and restraint and do not be provoked under any circumstances. Coolly discuss your viewpoint with a smile. If asked something you do not know, candidly admit your ignorance. Even if it's something vital, admit your ignorance and apologise for it. Your frankness will be appreciated.

If you are changing jobs, do not be critical of your present boss. Simply say the circumstances do not suit you or you seek better prospects.

The interviewer will not disclose whether you have been selected or not, but before concluding the interview you may be asked if you would like to ask anything in particular. Avail of this opportunity to clarify doubts about the job, the responsibilities, the benefits, etc. Be brief and specific. Before leaving, politely thank the interviewer.

❏ ❏ ❏

48

Etiquette of Changing Jobs

It is natural for young people to seek a new job and better prospects after some time. Do not change jobs just because others are doing so. Employers regard those who change jobs too often as unstable. When you find a better opening, study it thoroughly before taking it up. Consider both the pros and cons of changing jobs. Sometimes the increase in package may only be illusory.

To justify a change of job, there should be an increased salary, more responsibility, better chances of promotion, and lots of job satisfaction. You must give due notice to your present employer before leaving. But only do so after you have received a firm offer or appointment letter from the new employer. If the new employer desires a clearance certificate from the last employer, your present employer may wish to know why you are leaving. Be honest. Tell him you are seeking more responsible positions. Do not say you are unsatisfied with the current work conditions.

Most employers specify the salary and scale offered. Sometimes the matter is open to negotiation between the employer and the candidate. When changing jobs, it should not be difficult to relate the expected salary to the one you are already receiving. If unsure, make prior inquiries about what the job is worth by studying advertisements for similar jobs or through people working in similar posts. When asked, demand a salary accordingly. Never show indecision in these matters. If the employer finds you worthy of the amount you ask for, he will pay it. If you are capable and the difference is nominal, he will explain his stand to you.

In any job, you must create goodwill. Never close the doors when you leave. Always leave scope to return, perhaps to a better position. Good etiquette always pays rich dividends.

49

Etiquette at Meetings

Thousands of meetings are held daily with large sums of money and manpower spent. Unfortunately, most of these achieve nothing. To organise a successful meeting, be sure about certain things.

Is the meeting necessary? When in doubt, do not hold it. Only hold the meeting when there is a specific purpose.

Only well-planned meetings achieve their aim.

Has the meeting been properly announced? Were proper invitations sent to all participants? Has the agenda been circulated? Are all arrangements in place? For a successful meeting, ensure all these issues have been dealt with positively.

Meetings must begin bang on time. Discuss the agenda item-wise. Have writing slips and pens placed at every seat for notes. All relevant material pertaining to the discussion must be readily available. There must be no interruptions during the meeting. The receptionist must be told that no calls should be put through during the meeting, except if it is an emergency. All cell phones must be switched off. If refreshments are to be served, these must be arranged in advance and served either before the meeting or after it.

The minutes of the meeting must be appropriately recorded. If necessary, these can be circulated to the participants later. End the meeting on time. Punctuality reflects good etiquette.

❏ ❏ ❏

50

Etiquette at Public Meetings

Sometimes it is necessary to attend public meetings. You could be part of the audience, an active participant, a speaker, or the person introducing the speaker or assigned to present a bouquet or gift to the special guest. You could even be presiding over the public meeting. Whatever your role, you need to maintain good etiquette.

As part of the audience your responsibility lies in being a gracious guest who does not disturb the proceedings by talking, using a cell phone or loitering around the venue.

If you are presiding over the meeting, your responsibilities begin before the meeting and end only when everyone is gone. Acquaint yourself with the specific purpose of the meeting. Ensure all arrangements are in place. Ensure the loudspeaker system is working fine. As the president you may need to welcome special guests and the audience, and also brief them about the purpose of the meeting. At the end, you may need to give concluding remarks before the final vote of thanks.

If you have a special responsibility like introducing a guest speaker, or presenting a bouquet or garland, ensure that the bouquet or garland is readily available. If you are entrusted with the responsibility of introducing a speaker to the audience, take the proper bio-data of the person beforehand. Even if you only have to read this, ensure you have read it several times before the meeting. Do not slip over words or pronunciation. Keep introductions short.

If you are a speaker at the meeting, you hold a special responsibility. Accept a speaking assignment only if you are up to the task. Inquire in advance how long the organisers expect you to speak. Prepare yourself for that duration only. If it is a 15-minute talk, conclude it in 15 minutes, not 20 or 30 minutes. Exceeding the allocated time disturbs the entire schedule, embarrassing the organisers. More speakers are guilty of this one fault.

If you speak extempore, prepare well in advance. Organise your thoughts. Highlight important points. Practise before you deliver the speech. Once you are through, conclude the talk with a "thank you" and return to your seat.

When the speaker is at the podium, water or refreshments must not be served. These must only be given after the speaker concludes. Ensure nobody disturbs the meeting either by speaking or with children running about.

Thanksgiving at the end of the meeting should be brief. The correct etiquette at meetings will ensure their success.

51

Etiquette with the Family Doctor

Everyone needs a family doctor. It is important to have a good relationship with him. You may sometimes need him in an emergency. Note your doctor's telephone numbers on the first page of your personal telephone directory or diary. When you need to consult him, fix an appointment. Disturb him at home only if there is an emergency.

When you reach the clinic, register your presence with the doctor's assistant or the receptionist. Do not be impatient. Doctors are busy people. Everyone who visits a doctor has a health problem. The person he is examining may have a problem more serious than you.

If you have a problem where the doctor will need to examine you, wear clothes that are easy to take off. Tell him your problem in detail. Do not be shy about it or expect him to guess what your problem is. Only after hearing and examining you will he be able to diagnose your problem.

If the doctor suggests any tests to be conducted at a pathology laboratory, enquire about the laboratory he would recommend. Also inquire if you need to take any precautions before the test like not eating or drinking anything.

Maintain a record of your visits to the doctor by keeping his prescriptions in a file. Even if you feel fine, it is good practice to get a routine examination once a year. This way the doctor can immediately guide and help you.

❑ ❑ ❑

52

Etiquette in a Hospital

People visit hospitals for two reasons – when one needs special medical attention or when one visits a relative or friend who has been hospitalised. In both cases, one must observe certain etiquette.

Medical staff will treat you as encouraged to.

As a patient, do not be difficult. Just as in other professions, nurses discuss patients and classify them either as cooperative or difficult. Each category gets the attention they deserve. As a patient, you are in hospital for a particular purpose. The medical staff knows that. You are a part of their work. Your cooperation makes their work easier. They show their appreciation through kindness. You can then return home sooner. If you act difficult, or are impatient, you become a personal challenge to them. They will then tackle you in the way they deem best.

If you have a private room, you will have some liberties. In a common room or ward, you will need to be considerate about other patients. If you are uncomfortable, others can be equally so. When you ring the bell for the nurse's attention, do not become impatient. She is responsible for several patients. Allow her some time to come to you. The hospital food may not be to your taste and liking. Yet, you have to accept it. If you do so with a smile, you will be happier. If you grumble, it is your problem. Report it to the hospital authorities, only if there is something serious to be aggrieved about.

It is not customary to tip hospital staff. It is not necessary to give gifts either. The housekeeping staff and the sweeper may be tipped as a gesture of appreciation, when necessary.

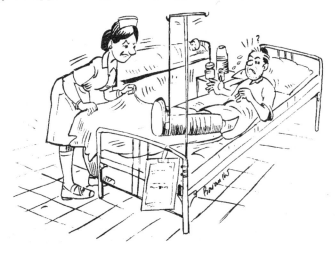

As a patient, please be patient.

All hospitals have visiting hours. Visit a hospital only during those hours. If you are suffering from a cough, cold or fever, avoid going to the hospital even as a visitor. You could pass on an infection to the patient. If you need to go, keep away from the patient. Children should not be taken to the hospital.

They run the risk of catching an infection there. Besides, they can act rowdy in the hospital, running up and down corridors, disturbing patients and the hospital staff. Silence is important.

Maintain silence in hospitals.

The purpose of your visit to the hospital is to express concern and inquire about the patient's health. If the patient is serious, you could inquire about his or her welfare from relatives in attendance. If the patient is not serious, after a brief meeting, maintain a distance. Do not talk too much or put the patient under strain by asking for too many details. Keep your visit to the hospital as short as possible.

❑ ❑ ❑

53

Etiquette of Writing Letters

"Letters are those winged messengers that can fly from east to west on embassies of love."

– Howell

At some time or the other, everyone needs to write a letter. Millions of letters are written everyday, crossing national and international borders with vital messages, and seeking a response. Some letters achieve their purpose. Many do not. If more people understood the need for writing effective letters, trade and business would grow manifold.

While some learn the art of writing letters quickly, others are slow learners. However, everyone can learn to write a good letter. So can you. The basic purpose of all letters is the same – to convey a particular message. Most letters fail because the message is not worded correctly. Even when it is, the presentation may be shoddy.

The letter is your messenger. It can work effectively only if it represents you well. A good letter must leave a lasting impression on the recipient's mind.

If you want your letters to be effective, use the best paper. Have a neat letterhead, displaying your name, address and other details. A professionally designed letterhead is best. When writing the letter, begin by writing the date on the top right side of the paper, just under the address. If it is a formal letter, you will need to write the name and address of the recipient, along with his designation, if necessary.

Begin the letter with a salutation, such as *Dear Sir*, or *Dear Mr Sharma*. Use the surname, not the first name. If the letter is informal, you could then begin simply by writing, *My dear Satish*.

The main body of the letter follows this. Now, identify the exact purpose of the letter. In putting the matter into words, remember the four Cs. The matter must be clear, concise, courteous and convincing.

You could also follow the ABC of letter writing. A is for drawing attention, B for brevity and C for convincing. A business letter may be closed with a complimentary close like *Yours faithfully*, if you began the letter with *Dear Sir*, or with *Yours truly*, or *Yours very truly*, if you opened the letter with *Dear Mr Sharma*. Personal letters can be closed with *Yours sincerely*.

You could then send the letter by post or courier, although most businesses prefer to use courier services, since they are comparatively cheap now and assure delivery within a day or two in most cases, unlike postal letters, which take much longer, sometimes never reaching their destination.

It is proper etiquette to respond to all letters you receive. E-mail has made things easier and faster. But in normal business where letters are kept on record, we cannot dispense with letter writing altogether. Even in personal relationships, letters will continue to play a role, as everyone does not have access to computers and e-mail.

❑ ❑ ❑

54

E-mail Etiquette

Computers in offices and homes and the mushrooming of cyber cafes have made e-mail communication very popular. People are even sending inter-office communications and letters through e-mails, rather than the conventional letter.

E-mail is a shortcut to the conventional letter. You do not need a letterhead, paper or envelope. Nor bother about using postage stamps or visiting the post office. You can even do away with the formalities of a conventional letter. Just sit down at the computer, open a file, write your message and send this via e-mail. The process is so fast that if the recipient is sitting at his computer, within the next few minutes you could have a response to your letter! Neither does it matter that the recipient lives in another part of the world.

As in all other forms of communications, however, etiquette and good manners are important even in e-mails. Most people have acquired e-mail addresses through some free service providers. These addresses are flouted on their stationery and visiting cards to impress others. However, with no personal computer, many rarely check their mail, visiting a cyber café occasionally to do so. But would you open the letterbox outside your home only once a month? No! Likewise, please check e-mail daily, particularly if your e-mail address is on the stationery.

When sending e-mail, people do away with several conventional practices like using capital letters, ensuring grammatical correctness, using proper punctuation and similar usage. Instead, they use abbreviations to write messages faster. It is proper to write short messages. Also, use lower case letters. Using all capitals is akin to shouting. Use this only if you need to emphasise something.

You can send attachments, if necessary. Do ensure these are not very big. Large mails are difficult to download. Besides, if not downloaded in time, the mailbox can get choked, creating problems for the recipient.

Do not forward all kinds of unsolicited mail to others. Such mail is referred to as Spam. This is irritating and can inconvenience and waste the recipient's time. Do not pass on e-mail addresses of friends and acquaintances to others without permission. This may result in their getting Spam mail.

Send mail only to the concerned person(s). Do not send copies to everyone you *think* would find it interesting. Address your mail to the persons from whom you expect a response by writing their names in the 'To:' box. Copies can be sent to others directly connected with the message, but do not need to respond, by putting their addresses in the 'Copy to:' box.

Do not create or forward chain mail. No one has ever been blessed with luck or received money by sending e-mail. Chain mail increases Internet traffic, slowing down the service. It also irritates recipients.

Hackers may forward virus-loaded mail to you. Never open mail from strangers, particularly when the subject is vague or mischievous. Many gullible people have fallen prey to such mail, suffering great loss through virus infections of the hard disk.

Also ensure that your personal computer is virus free. Many viruses lie dormant in the PC and are then transmitted through e-mail without your ever realising it. Follow proper etiquette and you will never have problems with e-mail.

❏ ❏ ❏

Freedom from Thought

—Ashok Gollerkeri

Don't let your Negative thoughts rule you

The book contains 50 spiritual essays which focus on joys and sorrows, triumphs and tragedies, spontaneity and complexities of human life. It also focuses on the universal nature of the challenges of human life, transcending all man-made barriers. Ashok examines the eternal thirst for lasting peace and joy, and the nature of the journey for self-discovery. A single reading of the book will transform your life. You will start realising how fortunate you are to have the gift of life and possess all that you do, rather than hanker for what you don't have!

Demy Size • Pages: 168
Price: Rs. 120/- • Postage: Rs. 20/-

Freedom from Negative Thoughts

—Guy Finley

Imagine how your life would flow without the weight of those weary inner voices constantly convincing you that "you can't", or complaining that someone else should be blamed for the way you feel. The weight of the world on your shoulders would be replaced by a bright, new sense of freedom. Fresh, new energies would flow. *You could choose to live the way YOU want.*

In **Freedom from Negative Thoughts**, Guy Finley reveals hundreds of celestial, but down-to-earth, secrets of Self-liberation that show you exactly how to be fully independent and free of any condition not to your liking. Even the most difficult people won't be able to turn your head or test your temper. Enjoy solid, meaningful relationships founded in conscious choice — not through self-defeating compromise.

Learn the secrets of unlocking the door to your own Free Mind. Be empowered to break free of any negative pattern, and make the discovery that who you really are is already everything you've ever wanted to be.

Demy Size • Pages: 166
Price: Rs. 120/- • Postage: Rs. 20/-

From Despair to Joy

—A.P. Sharma

Familiar Ways to Attain HAPPINESS

If happiness were a myth, the Buddha would never be able to accomplish it. Neither Ramkrishna, Vivekananda, Gandhi or others, who followed the road to impersonal love, would ever get it. The path leading to impersonal love is surely difficult, but nothing could be achieved without following the right path and the right means.

Happiness can be achieved if one can cultivate 'silence' of the mind. That silence can be attained by proper awareness. It can be reached by keeping the mind totally alert so that it acts like an observer who works without interfering with the others. Happiness can surely be obtained by keeping the mind's energy intact, without wasting it on insignificant matters. It can be obtained by meditation and prayers or by any informal procedure too, provided one is able to keep one's mind alert and free from mental fetters.

Demy Size • Pages: 104
Price: Rs. 80/- • Postage: Rs. 20/-

31 Mantras for Personality Development

—Abhishek Thakore

One tip a day to better yourself

Many of us have heard that the secret to a happy, joyous and successful life is to live in the present moment. Yet, acting out this simple truth eludes most of us. But the 31 practical tips and techniques in this book will teach you how to live each moment, each hour and each day to the fullest. By the simple expedient of making you follow one tip a day, each day the book takes you one step closer to becoming a better, more successful, happy and content human being.

Unlike other books on personal development and happiness, which are seemingly practical but not practicable, these steps can transform you into a new person within 31 days. All you have to do is read and practise just one tip everyday... beginning NOW!

And within a month, there will be a New You.

Demy Size • Pages: 104
Price: Rs. 100/- • Postage: Rs. 20/-

How to Remain Ever Happy

—M.K. Gupta

'*How to Remain Ever Happy*' is a masterpiece by the famous author of self-management books Er. M.K. Gupta, giving you countless practical tips for enjoying happiness in your day to day life.

The notable feature of the book is that you can start reading from any page as every tip is complete and independent in itself.

The author gives a message in short one or two page tips, which eliminates completely the scope of boredom or monotony. You will feel like flowing effortlessly with the matter while reading the book. Over 120 tips to make your life brighter and happier!

(also available in Hindi & Bangla)

Demy Size • Pages: 168
Price: Rs. 150/- • Postage: Rs. 20/-

77 Lesson to Remain Ever Positive

—M.K. Gupta

77 Lesson to Remain Ever Positive is a masterpiece by the well-known author of self-management books, Er. M.K. Gupta. This book has a vibe and style of its own which makes it completely different from the other books of this category. Once in hand, the reader flows effortlessly with the book feeling continuously the presence and vibrations of the author.

In this book, the author takes you on a journey towards freedom and happiness. According to him, freedom is the very fragrance of life. Freedom and happiness are very intimately linked with each other.

In the present book, the author gives various tips on freedom from various negative and undesirable traits from your personality. Once negativities disappear from your being, what remains is only positivity which will give you nothing but happiness.

Demy Size • Pages: 208
Price: Rs. 150/- • Postage: Rs. 20/-

Be Confident & Fearless

—Guy Finley

Reach New Heights in Your Journey to Higher Self-Awareness and Spiritual Growth

Life Changing Insights: "Freedom from what is unwanted by you begins with awakening to what is unseen *within* you."

True Encouragements: "Nothing can prevent the inwardly self-educating person from succeeding in life, because Wisdom *always* triumphs over adversity."

Self-Transforming Practices: "Meet each moment of your life with a wish *to understand* your inner condition, instead of looking for ways *to justify* it."

Higher Self-command: "We must cease our struggles to be victorious over our perceived enemy and struggle instead to see through the layered illustration that *who we really are* has anything to lose."

Demy Size • Pages: 240
Price: Rs. 175/- • Postage: Rs. 20/-

365 Recipes
That Will Make You
Think Positive

—Alan Cohen

As we scale the mountain of life, we could do so on our own or with the help of an inspired person or guru. Blind living makes the journey to the top of the mountain arduous, tiresome and seemingly never-ending. Guidance from an enlightened person makes the climb pleasant, enjoyable and fleeting. This book contains 365+ enlightened thoughts for each day of the year that could help you start your day on a positive note. At the end of the day, the book will help you review your day in the light of these principles.

"Each day's message includes a theme, a quote of wisdom, a parable or real-life anecdote, a prayer, and an affirmation. After reading the day's message, close your eyes for a few moments, and be with the prayer and affirmation. The spirit within you will expand miraculously as you nourish your inner being," says Alan Cohen.

By applying the principles contained within these pages, there will be tremendous healing, inspiration and positive changes in your life. You will be able to live life according to your heart and realise your true magnificence and potential.

Demy Size • Pages: 376
Price: Rs. 195/- • Postage: Rs. 20/-